West Cornwall

Rita Tregellas Pope

The name Tregellas was first recorded in 969AD.

The author has for many years belonged to the Society of Authors and the West Country Writers' Association. Since leaving teaching for writing she has produced educational material for Cornish publishers as well as books, articles and plays about Cornwall. These publications led to her being made a Bard of the Cornish Gorsedd 'for literary services to Cornwall'. This honour is the highest accolade which can be bestowed upon anyone loving the land west of the Tamar.

Inspired by her love of Cornwall, the author set about forming the Cornish Cultural Centre at Baldhu, Truro. As well as promoting Cornwall's heritage, this ecomuseum will exhibit the unique Tregellas Tapestry which she researched to tell the story of Cornwall. The author was nominated for the UK Woman of Europe Award 1995. She now has plans for more books — both fact and fiction — about Cornwall.

WEST CORNWALL

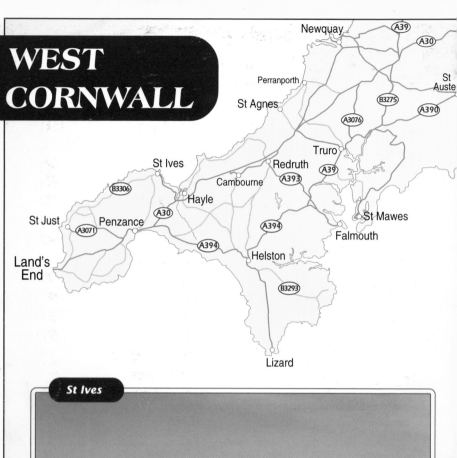

- Newquay (A39) (A30)
- Perranporth
- St Agnes
- St Auste
- (B3275) (A390)
- (A3076)
- Truro
- St Ives
- Redruth
- (A39)
- Cambourne (A393)
- (B3306)
- Hayle
- St Just
- (A30)
- (A3071) Penzance
- (A394) St Mawes
- Falmouth
- (A394)
- Land's End
- Helston
- (B3293)
- Lizard

St Ives

Acknowledgement

Landmark Publishing thanks Michael Bell of Bells Bookshop, Halifax, Yorks (01422) 365468 for supplying the material upon which the maps in this book are based.

CONTENTS

FEATURE BOXES

MAPS

• Gardens •

Magnificent as are the 80 acres of Heligan, abandoned to nature at the outbreak of the First World War and now uncovered from the overgrowth and restored as a living museum of nineteenth-century horticulture, it is only one of many lovely gardens, large and small, formal and informal that can be seen in West Cornwall throughout the year.

Mild winters lead to an early spring with wonderful displays of camellias, rhododendrons, azaleas and magnolias. Many sub-tropical species flourish and a number of gardens have special plant collections. Each year, from mid-March to the end of May, the Cornwall Festival of Spring Gardens takes place when many gardens open specially for the Festival, often in aid of local charities. Details of gardens participating and their opening times may be obtained from the Cornwall Tourist Board ☎ (01872) 274057.

Some of the most well-known gardens are highlighted in the book but the following will also reward the visitor:

Bosvigo, Truro
3 acres, mainly herbaceous, best in summer. Open March to September, Wednesday to Saturday, 11am–6pm ☎ (01872) 275774.

Burncoose Nurseries and Garden, Gwennap
36 acre woodland garden alongside working nursery. Open daily, all year ☎ (01209) 861112.

Carwinion, Mawnan Smith, Nr Falmouth
Valley garden with reference collection of bamboos.
Open daily all year, 10am–5.30pm ☎ (01326) 250258.

Creed, Grampound
5 acres including alpine and herbaceous gardens. Woodland walks.
Open daily mid-April to September, 10am–5.30pm ☎ (01872) 530372.

Fox Rosehill Gardens,
Melvill Road, Falmouth
2 acre garden, many exotic trees and shrubs. Free admission. Open daily, all year round, dawn to dusk ☎ (01872) 224355.

Japanese Garden,
St Mawgan Village
Water, Stroll and Zen gardens. Bonsai nursery. Open daily, all year, 10am–5.00pm ☎ (01637) 860116.

Lamorran House, St Mawes
4 acres. Water gardens. Palms and sub-tropical plants. Open first week April to end of September, Wednesday and Friday ☎ (01326) 270800.

Towan Camellias, Feock
Specialist Camellia nursery (some 200 varieties) in 3 acre garden setting. Open February to early May, Sunday to Friday ☎ (01209) 890252.

Trevarno Manor Gardens, Helston
Romantic 40 acre woodland gardens with lake, grotto and cascade.
Open daily all year, 10.30am–5pm ☎ (01326) 574274.

· Beach Guide ·

G olden sands, rocky coves, surf, cliffs, blue sea, bracing wind — everyone wants something different from a beach, and West Cornwall has all of these if you know where to look. No matter where one is on the peninsula, the sea and and wonderful beaches are not far away. Everyone will have their favourite and these are just a few suggestions.

Safe bathing beaches
Readymoney Cove, Fowey
Porthpean, St Austell
Gorran Haven, south of Mevagissey
Porthluney Cove, (by Caerhays Castle)
St Mawes
Gyllingvase; **Flushing**; **Swanpool**;
  Maenporth; all at Falmouth
Gunwalloe, near Helston
Praa Sands, west of Helston
Coverack, Lizard Peninsula
Poldhu, Mount's Bay
Marazion, nr Penzance
Porthcurno, south of Land's End
Sennen Cove, Land's End
Carbis Bay, St Ives
Gwithian, St Ives Bay
Trevaunance Cove, St Agnes

Surfing beaches
Long Rock, Penzance
Whitesand Bay, Land's End
Godrevy, Hayle

Rock pools can be found at:
Castle, nr Gyllingvase, Falmouth
Flushing, Falmouth
Godrevy, Hayle

Quieter beaches which may be more difficult to reach:
Towan, nr St Anthony Head
Vault, nr Gorran Haven
Prussia Cove and **Kenneggy Sands**,
  both at Mount's Bay
Peter's Point, Hayle
Penberth

Porthcurno Beach

Many beaches have lifeguards in attendance but whether this is the case or not, care should always be taken when bathing. Always keep well away from an estuary. Sea conditions can change rapidly and a system of warning flags is used to advise bathers.

When the red flag is flying, bathing is not permitted. Red-over-yellow flags at the water's edge mean bathe between these flags. Black and white flags at the water's edge indicate malibu board and surf craft areas.

Introduction

With the sea on three sides and the Tamar making the fourth boundary, Cornwall has always been almost an island and West Cornwall the most insular of all. So when wandering tribes from Europe arrived, they were able to enjoy a life of comparative peace — scarcely disturbed by the hordes who ravaged the rest of the mainland. That is why, with only wind and weather to affect them, so many Neolithic and Bronze Age monoliths and barrows remain.

Lamorna Cove

The richness of Cornwall's mineral deposits was not exploited until about 350BC when Iron Age tribes from Europe came in search of tin. The people of this fair-haired, blue-eyed race were tall and finely built, probably the originals of the 'giants' in Cornish folklore. They brought their knowledge of tin production with them as well as their culture and a completely new social structure.

Evidence of this important occupation is still to be seen in hill forts, cliff castles and the 'trevs' or settlements. The area of West Penwith, beyond Penzance, also retains low dry-stone walls and unique small fields — the latter having been cultivated continuously ever since Iron Age times.

Language & early settlement

The Tre-, Pol- and Pen- prefixes to family and place names which are so typical of Cornwall, also stem from that Iron Age period. For those tribes introduced the Indo-European Celtic language which, as Cornish, is the Brythonic branch. Although it seemed to die as the universally spoken tongue more than two centuries ago, it has now come out of hibernation. This revival, which began at the turn of the century, was inspired by dedicated men like Henry Jenner and Morton Nance.

Today the language is studied and spoken by linguists such as a former Bishop of Leicester, the Right Reverend Richard Rutt. It is an examination subject for school children and has recently become the first language in a number of homes. Many bards are fluent Cornish speakers and at their annual Gorsedd, awards are given for literary compositions in the Cornish tongue. Weddings, baptisms and other church services are also conducted in the language.

The much-maligned Druids were Celtic priests who, far from being mere growers of mistletoe, lovers of apples and makers of bonfires, were, in fact, the most highly respected scholars of their day. Men travelled across Europe to learn from them, early Greek was indebted to them and even the great Cicero paid tribute to their knowledge. People who laugh at their customs have only heard about the more sensational aspects and would doubtless be surprised to know that these same Druids were among the first of the so-called pagans to proclaim the doctrine of immortality.

Visitors interested in Roman remains will find few here. Romans did not settle in Cornwall but their merchants came here for tin, so the Romano-Cornish association was mainly through trade.

Arrival of Christianity

The next arrivals were of great importance, for they led the

Cornish people away from paganism to Christianity. These were holy men and women from Wales and Ireland who established their 'cells' near water — rivers, wells or streams. Many of these, previously objects of pagan worship, then became shrines and places of pilgrimage.

Today about a hundred holy wells still exist, most of them pleasant places to visit, others looked upon as serving a special purpose — turning the affections of a loved one in the right direction, for example!

Cornish churches (many near wells or water) are dedicated to those 'saints' and have names not seen in other English counties, such as St Gluvias, St Probus and St Petroc.

For centuries, Cornwall was entirely Celtic, but once the Anglo-Saxons had overcome England they turned to the west for further conquests. Here they met fierce resistance from Cornish chiefs or kings. One was Arthur, a Celtic ruler born in the late fifth century AD who led the last great Celtic battle against the Anglo-Saxons. The legends that grew up after his death and the medieval romances associated with his name, have so obscured the historical figure that it is now almost impossible to discover the truth about him.

By the end of the seventh century the Anglo-Saxons had conquered Devon but it was not till after AD926 that King Athelstan finally conquered the Cornish. A few Anglo-Saxons settled in Cornwall, mostly along the eastern border. Some ventured further and there is evidence of this in the scattering of non-Cornish place names found elsewhere — Wicca at Zennor is a good example.

From the Norman conquest

The Norman Conquest, however, did bring many changes. King William's custom of rewarding his barons with large estates held good in Cornwall — even to Land's End. The Domesday Book must have looked impressive with its accounts of groups of manors belonging to this or that Norman overlord. But many of the so-called manors were little more than small farmsteads or 'trevs' run by perhaps two people as they had been since Celtic times. In many cases, these homesteads are still farmed today — to be found almost hidden in a maze of narrow winding lanes.

Here West Cornwall has scarcely altered for centuries and those who would like to walk back in time need simply take the latest OS map and explore the narrow lanes of a remote parish. These lead to the very heart of West Cornwall. The castles the Normans built for defence — Launceston, Restormel and Trematon — also served to restore the sense of security the Cornish had lost since the Saxon conflicts.

By the mid-twelfth century, Cornwall was Europe's largest supplier of tin, and stannary towns grew up at places where tin was tested. Royal charters for markets and fairs also encouraged trade while the building of numerous collegiate and other churches resulted in a more settled way of life. By 1337, Cornwall was therefore a fitting land for King Edward III to bestow on his heir, the Black Prince.

At sea, as on land, Cornwall prospered. Her sailors and fishermen gained renown at home and abroad. Perhaps one of her proudest occasions was when Fowey sent forty-seven ships to help the king besiege Calais in 1346. This was nearly twice the number mustered by the City of London.

But sad times lay ahead. When the Reformation came, Cornwall's beautiful churches were stripped and most of her collegiate establishments closed. Men no longer travelled from Europe to study at Glasney Collegiate Church in Penryn and the place which might have been Cornwall's university is now remembered in a few scattered remains. The final blow came, however, when Bibles were printed in English — a language that Cornishmen did not want to understand and certainly could not read.

The tiny harbour at Coverack

1549 revolt

In an effort to preserve their culture, their way of life and their long heritage, the people rebelled. Many lost their lives in the 1549 revolt, but in vain. From then on the language began to decline. There is a saying in Cornish — *An lavar goth, yu lavar gwyr*. It means: 'He who loses his tongue (his language) shall lose his land.' And that was so, for as the language faded so did the customs and the essence of the nation. But Cornwall's identity was never completely overwhelmed and is still to be found today — very easily recognised.

Tin mining

With the passing of time, the Cornish learned to appreciate the diversity of riches which lay at their feet, for not only was the granite itself of incalculable value, but also the treasures hidden within the actual rock. Tin production continued for centuries but the massive copper deposits were not mined until about 1700. Then came William Cookworthy's china clay find at Tregonning and St Austell in the mid-eighteenth century with the Rev William Gregor's discovery of titanium at the end of it.

Prosperity returned briefly, however, in the eighteenth and nineteenth centuries when underground mining came into its own. The inventions of great Cornishmen like Richard Trevithick, Michael Loam and Goldsworth Gurney, enabled shafts to be sunk deep into the ground and even under the sea bed so that the increasing number of engine houses transformed much of the landscape.

Fortunes were made and lost almost overnight but Cornwall faced a major disaster once again when cheap surface tin was imported from Malaya. This time miners emigrated to look for work. Many settled in Canada, Australia, South Africa, Tasmania and the United States which often meant that whole families died out and Cornwall's glory faded again.

But there is much of the phoenix in this land. Its story has always been influenced by the rocks of its landscape and its coast. Granite has been the source of shelter in life and protection in death; of prosperity with tin and copper and more recently, china clay. Some feel that Cornwall's granite stones are only subjects for artists and photographers but scientists with vision have already begun to realise the great potential of this vast treasure store. The first dish scanners ever used for inter-satellite communication were built on the firm foundation of granite in the Lizard Peninsular.

Ancient place names

Once they are across the Tamar, motorists are soon aware of a subtle change in the atmosphere of the countryside through which they are driving. This can be noticed as they pass groups of granite farm buildings or cottages often built against the shelter of a hilly slope and it is these 'trevs' or homesteads that reflect the way of life in West Cornwall since Celtic times.

'Tre', 'Pol' and 'Pen' are first syllables which appear on many signposts as the road heads west. 'Lan' and 'Men' are other indications that this land is both Celtic and ancient.

For the 21ˢᵗ century visitor

Throughout the year there is an abundance of entertainment with festivals, plays, music and dance to be seen everywhere. The venues range from the unique Minack Theatre in the west, the solemn Gorsedd ceremony in a different open-air site each year, to local arts centres, National Trust properties and halls in every village.

At any place in West Cornwall — town, village or hamlet — visitors will be certain to discover outstanding talent in arts and crafts. It is not only artists who abound but others skilled in weaving, pottery, woodcarving, metal work, leather work and the creation of stained glass items. The list is endless and fascinating to the tourists whose visits form such an important part of West Cornwall's economy.

The Cornish language has its living presence in place names everywhere. Perhaps this is one reason why there is such an increase in the number of people studying it. Celtic associations are to be found across the Continent, place names with a Celtic prefix appear even on maps of Slovenia.

The geography of West Cornwall offers 'much in little' for visitors who come for an activity holiday. There is rock and cliff climbing at coastal resorts while sailing, surfing, windsurfing, diving, canoeing and fishing are also to be found there. Golf, walking and riding can be enjoyed throughout West Cornwall too.

Sub-tropical Cornwall

As the Gulf Stream washes the Cornish coast it is not surprising that sub-tropical and some tropical species flourish in West Cornwall.

William and Thomas Lobb were the first plant hunters sent overseas for a commercial firm and although some of their discoveries are not well-known, many of the plants they found now thrive in their native West Cornwall.

Those interested in such matters should note the Lobb Garden at Baldhu and the William Lobb section of Fox Rosehill Gardens in Falmouth. A visit to the Lizard Countryside Centre at Trelowarren will not only be pleasant but very informative. The granite mass which is the Lizard Peninsula is the reason for the unique flora and fauna to be found there.

Archaeology, painting, visits to the many lovely gardens and various summer workshops are only some of the holiday pastimes which visitors can enjoy. So those who travel to West Cornwall to see the eclipse in 1999 will also be able to discover what lies at the very heart of this ancient land. The only difficulty is deciding how to spend the precious time.

• TRURO •

The exact meaning of the name Truro is uncertain, though of the suggested 'settlement near water', 'three roads' and 'three rivers', possibly the last is the most likely. The 'three rivers' were the Allen, Kenwyn and a third, long lost under Tregolls Road where the A39 enters the city from the east.

Truro Cathedral

The **Assembly Rooms** by the cathedral has a fine façade worthy of attention, as is Ralph Allen Daniell's Mansion House in Prince's Street. He was wealthy enough to use Bath stone and have the oak specially carved by craftsmen from the local French prisoner of war camp. The date 1792 is engraved on the roof. Merchants like William Lemon built elegant houses on both sides of Lemon Street, named after him, and looking down on them is a monument to Richard Lander. He discovered the source of the River Niger and, in 1830, was the first holder of the Royal Geographical Society's Gold Medal.

The ordinary houses, too, are worth more than a passing glance. Look for strangely shaped roofs, old porticos, decorated façades, narrow, pointed windows and emotive names like Tanyard Court, Tippett's Backlet, Pydar Street and Coombes Lane — recalling the great days of Truro's wool trade. St Nicholas Street may not seem unusual, but here the merchants' houses and warehouses were cheek by jowl with the Guildhall of St Nicholas, probably extending across Boscawen Street down to Lemon Quay itself.

The present car park is where ships anchored while waiting for their cargoes. Today at the Quay, across the A39, pleasure boats berth in the summer and run weekday boat trips down the Fal.

Most Cornish towns have narrow passages between houses. These are 'opes' — pronounced 'ops'. Truro is no exception and Squeezeguts Alley is perhaps the smallest and most awkward; Cathedral Lane is another 'ope'.

Designed in Gothic style by J.L. Pearson, **Truro Cathedral** was constructed 1880–1910, and consecrated in 1887. The west porch niches facing High Cross have figures of kings and bishops. Look out for the beautifully carved memorial to one of the Robartes family of Lanhydrock who died in the Great War. It is near the south-

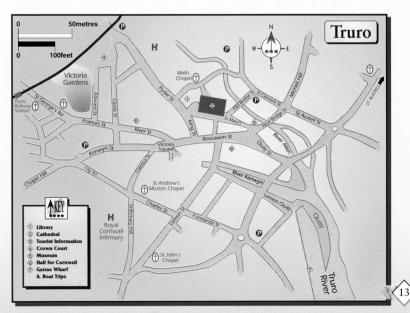

west corner. There is also a cathedral bookshop for books and souvenirs and the Chapter House where you can get refreshments.

The then Prince of Wales laid the foundation stone of the cathedral on 20 May 1880. It was the first to be built in Britain since St Paul's. Truro, however, had become a city in 1877 when Bishop Benson was enthroned in St Mary's parish church. This was later demolished, except for the south aisle, which was incorporated into the new building. The three-spired towers are interesting in their dedications. The central one (Victoria) was given in 1901 as a memorial to the Queen's life, and 9 years later, another local benefactor gave the two western towers — Edward and Alexandra. Altogether an unusual building, its Gothic style gives the city a continental look.

Its Willis organ is famous and interesting features include memorials to 'Q' (Sir Arthur Quiller-Couch, the essayist) and the missionary Henry Martyn. Notice the Bath stone reredos representing Christ's sacrifice, the window showing John Wesley preaching at Gwennap Pit and the painting *Cornubia* by John Miller. The first bishop, Edward White Benson originated the service of Nine Lessons

Royal Institution of Cornwall Museum and Art Gallery

River Street, Truro
Exhibitions of Cornish history, archaeology, ceramics, costume, minerals and natural history. Has a library of Cornish books for members and an interesting art gallery. Facilities include pavement café and large gift/bookshop.
☎ (01872) 272205.
Open: 10am–5pm not Sundays or Bank Holidays.

and Carols here in 1880 and, after serving in Truro for 7 years, he was translated to Canterbury.

There is much to see in the **Royal Institution of Cornwall** (founded in 1818) which is both an art gallery and a museum. On display is a variety of material connected with life in the region since earliest times; the mining section is unusually fine. During the summer season there is generally an exhibition of special interest.

Speciality Foods

Truro is small compared with other cities, but it takes time to explore it fully. The Pannier Market is an exciting place — the cheese stall is exceptionally good and adjoining shops have their own specialities. Truro's restaurants are numerous, varied and of a high standard with the Wig and Pen, at the bottom of Castle Street, a reminder of the city's nineteenth-century cultural gatherings.

• TIN MINING COUNTRY •

The great men of Truro made fortunes in tin during the eighteenth and nineteenth centuries, but it had been 'streamed' in the surrounding districts long before Truro became an important trading centre, so it is interesting to look at those old mining areas. The Truro to Falmouth A39 road down Arch Hill, goes under the track of a railway before climbing the hill to Playing Place — once the site of a theatre-in-the-round. At the Playing Place roundabout is the entrance to Killiow Golf Park.

The preserved winder or whim at East Pool Mine, Pool, near Redruth, is now in the care of The National Trust

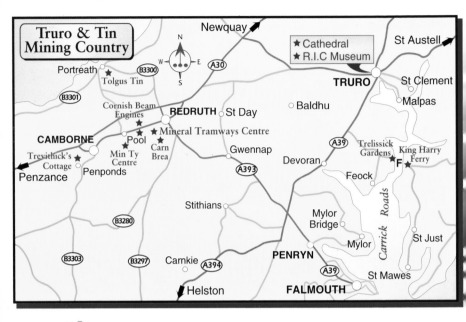

Truro & Tin Mining Country

★ Cathedral
★ R.I.C Museum

Killiow Golf Park

Just 3 miles from Truro off A39
18-hole parkland course. Floodlit golf driving range.
☎ 01872 270246.

Carnon Downs looks like a bungalow suburb, but hides much mining history. Its much-needed by-pass is now complete and at the roundabout take the left-hand exit for **Come-to-Good**, a misleading name which has quite a different meaning. The thatched Quaker Meeting House of 1710 is called after its location *Cwm-ty-quite* — Cornish for 'the House of the Coombe in the Woods,' appropriate for this attractive building still in use.

Feock church has an interesting lych-gate with a slate-hung upper storey and expensive properties beyond the village straggling down to Restronguet Point beside the Carrick Roads. Before Tudor times a passenger ferry, which functioned at the turn of this century, took travellers from Truro through Mylor to Penryn and Falmouth.

Across the narrow water is the thatched **Pandora Inn**. Originally called The Ship, it was renamed when its captain returned from sailing with Bligh of the *Bounty* to capture the mutineers. On the return voyage, the vessel — the *Pandora* — foundered and though its captain brought home some prisoners he was dismissed from the service. He then bought this inn and named it after his lost ship.

Timber from Scandinavia

At **Point**, Restronguet Creek is joined by the Carnon River, a bird sanctuary and a place of beauty. Once it was a prosperous mining port with a smuggling reputation as well. Tin has been streamed in the Carnon River since the days of pre-history, and in the Middle Ages, ore for export from the inland mines was brought here on mules and horses. In 1826 the Redruth and Chacewater Railway opened, the stretch from Devoran to Point still retaining horse-drawn wagons: part of this track can still be seen.

Great schooners from Scandinavia anchored there, unloading timber which was taken on barges to Perran Wharf. The Norway Inn is a reminder of those days. There are still bollards and wooden wharves at **Devoran** and the old weighbridge gate remains at the junction where the Bissoe road leaves the A39.

Beyond the Norway Inn, a road winds away to Perranwell and opposite are the buildings of Perran Foundry (1799) recalling the days when the Fox family established an industrial site there. The machinery was of high quality and European nations bought it: they supplied the world's largest steam engine to the Netherlands for draining the Haarlem Meer.

Turn right over the railway bridge at **Perranwell** and drive along Grenna Lane. There you will overlook the Carnon Valley and perhaps imagine what it was like when mining was at its peak.

Then beyond Perranwell and Frogpool, **Gwennap** village lies in peaceful beech woods, deceptively quiet now, yet once the heart of a region which yielded more copper and tin than any other place in the old world. Gwennap Pit is not in the village, but is near **Busveal**, reached by turning off the A393 Falmouth to Redruth road at the Fox and Hounds, one of the many inns where a service is held and produce auctioned for charity at harvest time.

The road twists and climbs above the derelict expanse of the now silent mines: Crofthandy, Goon Gumpus, Creegbrawse, Tolgullow and others with Celtic names. The men who worked there often died young and left widows with families. Others fell ill and were unable to work. Wesley's message from the Pit and elsewhere brought hope to these people because, as he wrote, 'The more I conversed with the believers in Cornwall, the more I am convinced that they have sustained great loss for want of hearing the doctrine of Christian Perfection clearly and strongly enforced.'

Gwennap Pit was probably formed by the collapse of underground mining excavations. In 1806, circular terraces were cut for seating and since 1807, an annual service has been held there on Whit Mondays. Wesley, who visited Gwennap 18 times between 1762 and 1789, wrote of preaching in a

Gwennap Pit and Methodist Museum

Carharrack, Busveal, Redruth
Open: 9.30am–11.30am
on Tuesdays and
Thursdays.

hollow capable of containing many thousands of people. Gwennap Pit is certainly large and was central and ideal for his purpose whether it held hundreds or thousands. A museum of Cornish Methodism was opened near here in 1982.

Carharrack is a village of mining memories while nearby **St Day** was, in 1841, acknowledged to be the mining capital of Cornwall and its second largest parish (pop. 10,000). Both villages are on the Mineral Tramways Route. Once tin and copper ore reached ground level it was taken to the nearest port along tramways or railways. The Trevithick Trust is restoring them so that, as leisure trails they can be used for walking, cycling, horse riding and bird watching.

St Day also has another place in history. It was an important resting place for pilgrims en route to St Michael's Mount.

Killifreth engine house, beside the B3298 St Day-Scorrier road, is undoubtedly one of the most impressive industrial buildings remaining. It is near **Scorrier** where John Williams, the mining entrepreneur, built his fine mansion. At nearby **Chacewater**, formerly Chasewater, there are memories of Cornwall's first true railway.

Not quite two miles north-east along the A30 is **Blackwater**, the birthplace of John Passmore Edwards who built reading rooms and institutes for all workers, especially miners. His Reading Room there stands beside the main road; and almost every town in Cornwall owes its library to him. Altogether he was responsible for fifty-three benefactions from Newlyn to Dundee.

This section of the A30 has three important tumuli beside it, Two Burrows, Three Burrows and Four Burrows and one of the Midsummer Eve Bonfire ceremonies held by members of the Old Cornwall Society usually takes place at the last of these.

Two, Three and Four Burrows

Important prehistoric tumuli
Beside the narrow road S of B3277; beside A30 at junction of A30 and A390; beside A30 about 2 miles E of above.

From the A390 at Chacewater, minor roads lead to **Baldhu** (Black Mine) and **Wheal Jane Mine**, re-opened in 1970 as a modern mining complex but now closed. Visit **Baldhu Church** where churchyard memorials tell of the overseas journeys miners undertook to find work and there is a handsome stone commemorating Billy Bray. He is buried there but a small chapel nearby was actually built by this preaching miner. The surrounding area is one where mineral enthusiasts can explore ochre pits, arsenic works and similar remains. From here to Truro by way of the winding lanes of Penweathers there are walks and picnic places.

Moving west, away from the immediate area around Truro is **Wendron** and the **Poldark Mine** some three miles north of Helston, along the B3297. Here you can safely go underground and experience for yourself something of the past. Tin lodes, working machinery, and even dripping water help to recreate the mining age, with some of Richard Trevithick's instruments on display. Allow plenty of time here.

Poldark Mine

Wendron

A real mine to explore. Another world of tunnels, chambers and caves where old machinery is at work. Choice of three walk-in tours. Also museum of mining ephemera, picnic areas and undercover amusements for children. Part access for the disabled.
☎ (01326) 573173.
Open: 10am–5.30pm daily, end of March to end of November.

North once more, the bleak **Carnmenellis Moor** emphasises the mining atmosphere and a short climb to Hangman's Barrow and the Nine Maidens stone circle adds still more. This, too, is a place of many walks.

Nine Maidens/ Hangman's Barrow

Megalithic standing stones
Near junction of B3297 Wendron road and B3280 Praze-an-Beeble to Redruth road.

Nearby, **Stithians Reservoir** is a must for ornithologists, watersports enthusiasts and anglers but they should first obtain permission from South West Water.

The village of **Carnkie**'s disused engine houses have a melancholy beauty best viewed from the centre of the village and then in panorama from **Carn Brea**. Here is another place to visit whether you are artist, historian, birdlover or gourmet. Good coffee and full meals are served at the restored Carn Brea Castle. Come when gorse and heather are out, explore the top of the Brea, where you can sit and relax and, while admiring the view, perhaps wonder about the Neolithic families who once lived here. The 90ft granite monolith is a memorial to Francis, Lord de Dunstanville and Basset of Tehidy, erected in 1837.

Then find the path downhill to **St Euny**, Redruth Churchtown. Nearby Reswythen Bridge was made unstable in 1301 by the mining operations of Ralph Wenna and John de Treveyngy and their goods were confiscated to pay for the damage. In **Redruth** itself, in Cross Street, William Murdoch used his invention of gaslight for the first time in 1792. Murdoch House has been restored as a memorial to him.

If, however, you drive down to Carnkie village, take the uphill road to the junction at the top and follow the right hand road down to Penhallick. There, at Old Cowlin's Mill is the **Mineral Tramways Centre** with fascinating information about Cornwall's industrial heritage.

Mineral Tramways Visitor Centre

Old Cowlin's Mill, Carn Brea
Introduction to the footpath network which retraces the Mineral Tramway Routes. Exhibition, book and gift shop. Admission free.
☎ (01209) 612917.
Open: 10am–4pm all year, Sunday to Friday.

Sir Richard Tangye (1833–1905) was born at **Illogan** and became a national benefactor and a brilliant engineer. He instituted the Saturday half-holiday and also built machinery to raise Cleopatra's Needle on the London Embankment. He was inspired by a fellow-countryman, the neglected genius, Richard Trevithick (1771–1833).

Richar

If you come to **Camborne** near to 26 April you might be fortunate enough to join in the Trevithick Day celebrations — held close to that day — when people remember one of Cornwall's most colourful characters. The son of a mining engineer, he followed his own ways even while he was at school, paying little attention to lessons because he was absorbed in his own diagrams and calculations. He would not even learn to spell, yet could produce the correct answer to any mathematical problem six times faster than any adult.

When he left school officially, Trevithick refused to have anything to do with the mine administration affairs in his father's office and wandered about the underground workings, examining and studying everything. The miners appreciated his knowledge of the machinery and his skill as a wrestler made him a popular figure.

His invention — the high-pressure engine — so impressed the wealthy Cornishman, Davies Gilbert (later President of The Royal Society) that they grew to be close friends. On Christmas Eve 1801 Trevithick frightened the local people with his 'puffing devil' which carried ten

evithick

or more passengers even uphill (the model he made in 1797 is now in the Science Museum in London). Two years later he took a similar engine to London but had to bring it home because of financial difficulties.

There is no room here to tell more about the extraordinary career of this great man except to say that his high pressure locomotive predated Stephenson's *Rocket* by 12 years. Among his other inventions were the blast pipe, a ship propeller, screw propeller and central heating, yet the government flatly refused him any remuneration for his brilliant work. In desperation he turned to the New World but there met similar ups and down of fortune. Eventually he went to London and died while working at Dartford in Kent. Because of his penniless state he was buried in an unmarked grave but there is a tablet to his memory in the parish church, and windows in Westminster Abbey record his main achievements. His statue outside Camborne Library faces the street where he first put his theories into practice.

Pool has a fine Leisure Centre and it is a good place to spend a day enjoying sport or relaxing — sometimes plays are performed here, too. Beside the main road at Pool is a restored Cornish 'whim' engine or steam winding engine, while just north of this is a huge Cornish beam engine.

The whim raised copper ore from the East Pool Mine to the surface, while the beam engine pumped water out of the workings. These two engines are now in the care of the National Trust.

Camborne School of Mines Museum

Midway between Camborne and Redruth, the School of Mines houses a fine collection of minerals and rocks from Cornwall and many other parts of the world. ☎ (01209) 714866. Open: 9am–5pm Monday to Friday all year (except Bank Holidays)

The internationally famous Camborne School of Mines, housing a museum, is on the A3047, while just off the B3303 at **Penponds** is the cottage — now National Trust but not open to the public — where Trevithick lived for a great part of his life and perfected most of his inventions.

Cornish Beam Engines

Pool
Splendid working winding engine alongside the old A30 half-way between Camborne and Redruth.

Nearby and also open is the pumping engine house at Taylor's Shaft with its enormous 90 inch cylinder. Here too is the Cornwall Industrial Discovery Centre.
☎ (01209) 216657.

Open: 10am–5pm daily April to October.

The second of the two National Trust engines open to visitors at Pool.

· Traditional Food ·

With so much to see and do in West Cornwall, healthy appetites are very much the order of the day. What better then, than to sample the many traditional foods that can be found here. Seafood is wonderful from crabs, lobsters and shellfish to mackerel, pilchard and sole. Every harbour and cove will have at least a couple of boats bringing in fresh catches and specialist fish restaurants abound.

According to some people, the only food associated with Cornwall is a pasty. That is certainly not correct but few know that there can be at least ten fillings to this healthy 'convenience food', the traditional one being best steak, potato, onion, salt and pepper.

Originally baked for the miners to take to the depths of the mine for their mid-day meal, the pasty could have a savoury filling at one end and a sweet one at the other. The crimped edge was there for the miner to hold his pasty with his arsenic stained hands. The crust was then discarded to appease the mine spirits, if you take the romantic view, or to avoid arsenic poisoning if you are a realist. Whichever way you look at it, a delicious all-in-one meal was invented that is still enjoyed today.

Others however are eager to taste the clotted or scalded creams, made differently from cream produced in Devonshire. Queen Elizabeth I learnt about it from her sailors but probably did not know that it had to be eaten with splits — not scones. Not often met is a teatime delicacy named *thunder and lightning*; this is splits spread with golden syrup and topped with clotted cream. The word clotted comes down from 'clout', a thick piece of leather. So the cream served with your tea should be like a thick crust (or leather) not a semi-solid cream. Do not complain, however, because true scalded cream is rarely found except in farmhouses.

Dairy produce used to be plentiful in Cornwall and junket was a popular dessert. In traditional households today, junket topped with cream is one of the May Day customs still observed. Look too for Cornish cheeses, made on the farm.

According to local tradition, saffron cake should only be eaten indoors. Rarely found outside Cornwall this is a yeast bun delicately flavoured and coloured with saffron, obtained from the stigmas of the crocus flower. Heavy or 'hevva' cake is quite different, made from flour, sugar, butter/lard, currants and cream and scored in a fish-net pattern.

Star-Gazey pie must surely be unique. Pilchards are baked in a pastry crust with the heads projecting from a hole in the centre. Traditionally this pie is eaten on 23 December in Mousehole to celebrate Tom Bawcock's Eve.

Good eating places are everywhere, offering local Cornish produce — new potatoes, fresh vegetables, seafood, strawberries, cream and meat — to give the best of both old and new regional specialities. Make the next visit a food tasting one and add to it by drinking local beer, Cornish mead or wine from one of the vineries.

A boat trip up Carrick Roads near to Falmouth

The Roseland Peninsula includes the west side of Veryan Bay and Gerrans Bay, and is easily explored from Truro during a fairly long but lovely drive. Take the A3078 where it turns off the A390 between Tresillian and Probus. It crosses the Tregony bridge where the left turn leads up to the now quiet village with its wide central street.

Tregony was once a bustling port and had a castle, a medieval market and a thriving wool factory. Even when the river silted up and trade declined, it was still a society meeting place. In the late nineteenth century, the learned Powder Book Club held meetings there for the improvement of local ladies, but no such excitements now remain. Little is left of former glories except the fourteenth-century church of **St Cuby** with its slate tower and the handsome seventeenth-century clock tower which was rebuilt in 1895. Tregony is now a place of the past, recalling when ships unloaded ceramics, glass and wine then sailed away with leather, wool and tin.

From Tregony, high-banked, narrow lanes lead to **Portholland**, a harbour of two coves, east and west. There is a fine cliff path to **Portloe** but motorists lose the view temporarily as the road takes the inland route to this tiny port more used to horse and pony transport than motorised traffic. Parking halfway down the steep hill to the beach avoids unpleasant turns, but visitors to the comfortable seventeenth-century Lugger Inn, will find a park beside it. This village loses the sun very quickly, lying in the shadow of Jacka and Manare Points, but it is a pleasant place in the sunshine.

Some land here is owned by the National Trust including a considerable area along the cliff to **Nare Head**, where there is a viewing platform with a ramp for wheelchairs. One of the Trust walks is round the point from Caragloose to Camels Cove. At Kiberick Cove there is a small car park and a footpath to the secluded beach. Another walk from the same parking place is down the valley to Paradoe Cove beyond the Nare, returning via that fine headland — one of the least frequented in Cornwall.

After passing Crugillick Manor on the way to the A3078, there is a walk down the lovely wooded valley to **Pendower Beach**, another National Trust property. A disused lime-kiln is an interesting feature of this pleasant place. The great

Veryan's Roundhouses

Veryan is well known but still relatively unspoilt. The reasons for its fame are the unique roundhouses at each end of the village. Some say that a local vicar built two of them to keep the devil out and away from his daughters. Whatever the reason, the white, thatched cottages have a charm all their own. Inside the church, with its unusual dedication to St Symphorian, lies Admiral Kempe, notable for sailing round the world with Cook and scaling Quebec Heights with General Wolfe.

tumulus (Cornwall's largest) at nearby **Carne Beacon** is said to be the burial mound of King Geraint who built Dingerin Castle where the Gerrans road leaves the A3078. It is believed that his tribesmen rowed his body, in a golden boat with silver oars, across the bay to be burned and buried at Carne.

The church and art gallery at **Gerrans** village offer different, but equally good, attractions for visitors.

From here is a walk of about 4 miles along the coast path to St Anthony Head, the eastern arm of Falmouth harbour. This superb route offers unsurpassed panoramic views on every side until reaching Zone Point and the lighthouse built in 1808 for J.B.

Trevanion. The headland has been fortified since Napoleonic days, was under military occupation during World War II and then bought by the National Trust in 1959. There is wheelchair access to the viewpoint.

Another exploration of the Roseland Peninsula is shorter and could last either an afternoon or a day. In early July, a signpost at Tresillian Bridge invites fruit lovers to pick strawberries at Fentongollan Farm. This is a pleasant task in good weather as the farm is set high over woodlands and rolling fields. Follow the road to **St Michael Penkevil** — a handful of cottages round the church with the great gates of Tregothnan proclaiming it as private property. On certain

The church at St Just-in-Roseland, situated in a lovely churchyard-cum-garden beside the peaceful creek

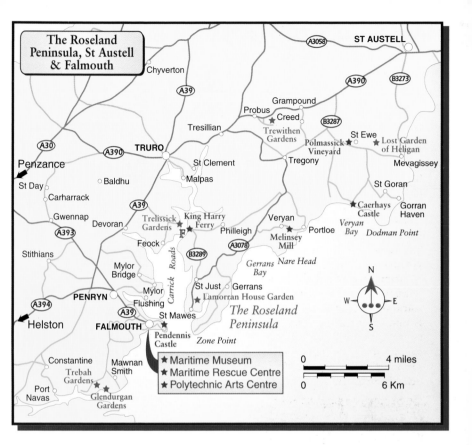

The Roseland Peninsula, St Austell & Falmouth

days in early summer, Lord and Lady Falmouth open their gardens for charity (☎ 01872 520325 for dates). Visitors enjoy the magnificent shrubs and see some of the mansion's 365 windows.

In 1319, the church was an important archpresbytery (a college with four chaplains). A handsome building, restored in 1863-5 it has an interesting feature in the second altar on the upper floor of the tower, an old tradition in churches dedicated to St Michael.

Leaving the churchtown, take the first lane on the right through beautiful **Lamorran Woods** which leads to **Ruan Lanihourne**. This is a haven for birdwatchers and there is also a 4-mile walk beside the river, where ships once sailed to Tregony.

There are walks to **Philleigh** where the old Rectory, a fine early Georgian house with an elegant slate-hung façade is worthy of more than a passing glance. Set nearby in Cornish elms is the church with its unusual dedication to St Filius.

Resist the temptation to drive straight to King Harry Ferry — leave that until later — but watch the last times of sailing! Go on to **St Just-in-Roseland** where the church, in its creekside setting of tropical trees, is possibly unrivalled for beauty of position. At the water's edge of St Just Pool, ships' figureheads or specialised work for the QEII used to be made.

St Mawes Castle

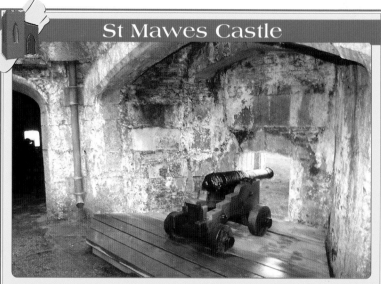

Described as Henry VIII's most decorative fort. Colourful gardens and lawns to the sea. Unusual clover-leaf plan produced by a central tower with three semi-circular bastions. Small but interesting with ample parking.
☎ (01326) 270526.
Open: 10am–6pm (dusk if earlier) April to October daily and 10am–4pm November to March, Friday to Tuesday.

The A3078 eventually reaches St Mawes Castle and drops down into the village to follow the harbour round for the return journey. **St Mawes** is a sheltered place and a yachting paradise, particularly for the wealthy. **St Mawes Castle**, cared for by English Heritage, is a round tower, built by Henry VIII and probably enlarged by his son Edward in 1550. Its name is believed to have come from the hermit, St Mawes, St Mauditus or St Mause who effected cures with the water from a holy well. The grounds are pleasant — an ideal place to picnic and watch the various activities on the Carrick Roads.

The latest ferry glides smoothly across the Fal to **Trelissick**, another delightful National Trust property. The house is not open but the grounds are lovely in all seasons with rare shrubs and plants, extensive parklands, woods and farmland. The superb views include vistas of the Fal Estuary and Falmouth harbour. The Trust has made a nature trail round the grounds.

The thatched Punch Bowl and Ladle Inn at **Penelewey** dates from the eleventh century and is probably the only one with such a name. Cowlands Creek and Coombe are worth a detour to enjoy the birds, the creekside walks and the famous Kea plums. The lane joins the A39 Falmouth

Trelissick

The Carrick Roads from Trelissick Gardens

Near Feock
Gardens only but they have fine shrubs, including tender and exotic plants, and nature trails. Art and craft gallery, two restaurants and shop specialising in Cornish foodstuffs. Part disabled access.
☎ (01872) 862090. Gardens open March to November 10.30am–5.30pm, Monday to Saturday, 12.30pm–5.30pm Sunday (closes 5pm in March and October), woodland walks open all year.

to Truro road at **Calenick**, once the site of Cornwall's chief smelting house. All that remains of it is the handsome clock tower on the slate-hung Bridge House.

East of Veryan

This area too can be approached from Truro, leaving the city at the Trafalgar roundabout, by a road running past Radio Cornwall, the BBC's first purpose-built local radio station. The road follows the river to **Malpas** (Mopus).

At the end of the road there is a footpath to **St Clement**. Photographers love the old church and thatched cottages — the slate-hung upper room over the

lych-gate provides added interest. From here one of the Duchy's loveliest creekside paths leads to Pencalenick, where the A390 is rejoined for **Tresillian**. At the far end of this long village is the uniquely thatched Wheel Inn. The rolled wheel is something probably not seen on any other roof. Here history was made when the Civil War ended and the Royalist Lord Hopton capitulated to Fairfax after surrendering at the bridge. Fairfax Road beside the water commemorates the occasion.

You will need more than a day to explore the **Veryan area** and to visit some of the interesting places on the way, such as the Wheel Inn.

Follow the road, the A390, out of Tresillian and take the exit to **Probus**, which is now a quiet village but was once an educational centre. Now only its collegiate church and a road name, College Close, are left as reminders. The fine church tower is Cornwall's highest, at 123ft 6in, lovely with its finely carved granite. Recently restored and replaced outside the church is an attractive lamp standard erected to celebrate Queen Victoria's Diamond Jubilee.

Just east of Veryan is Melinsey Mill, a recently restored watermill where you can relax and enjoy your refreshments by the lovely mill pond.

Just past the village is Cornwall's **Demonstration Garden and Arboretum**. Keen gardeners can learn much there but it also has interesting displays and layouts in beautiful surroundings to delight the amateur. It is open throughout the year although at the time of writing there is some doubt about its continuing survival.

Probus Demonstration Garden and Arboretum

Probus
Plant centre, shop, café, wheelchair access.
☎ (01726) 882597.
Open: 10am–4pm,
April to October daily;
November to March
Monday to Friday only.

Just over 3 miles beyond lies **Grampound**, quietly at peace beside the rushing traffic, deceptively different from the bustling port

Melinsey Mill, near Veryan

of Norman times when the sea brought ships there. When silting began, a bridge over the Fal was built at that point and the town was given the name Grand-pont — known in 1299 as the Borough of Ponsmur, its Celtic name. Eventually maritime trading ended and the town declined slowly into the present peaceful village.

Halfway up the hill almost opposite its handsome clock tower are two thatched houses, the Manor and Cornwall's only **bark tannery** where visitors are welcomed but only by appointment (☎ 01726 882413). This is the place which provided skin for the hull and sails of Tim Severin's curragh *St Brendan*, which weathered a force eight gale and crossed the Atlantic safely in 1976, proving the theory of the author-historian captain who believed that St Brendan made the same crossing a good thousand years before Columbus — in an identical craft.

The second turning on the right, up the hill out of Grampound, winds narrowly to **St Ewe**, beautiful and almost unspoilt. The church, enclosed by trees, has old stocks inside — both merit a close look. Follow the hill down to **Polmassick**, cross the bridge and a few yards past the chapel is another of Cornwall's unexpected delights — a vineyard where wines are available. There are

walks round the vineyard and the nearby farm. Have some refreshments here and perhaps also buy a vine.

After Kestle is **Mevagissey**, one of the Duchy's oldest fishing ports. Its narrow streets and quaint shops, up the hills or by the quays, make it a captivating place. Watch the gulls and the fishing boats or go fishing. If it rains, there are always the **Model Railway** and **Museum** to enjoy.

World of Model Railways

Mevagissey
An unusual attraction offering a miniature world of nearly fifty trains. Collection of model locomotives and rolling stock. Children's layout at floor level. Model shop. Wheelchair access.
☎ (01726) 842457.
Open: from 10am, daily during summer, Sundays only in winter.

Park on the harbour quays and move for a while into a miniature world which has been featured on television. There is enjoyment here for the whole family.

Polmassick Vineyard

St Ewe
A thriving vineyard, planted on the slopes of the Luney Valley. Wines by the glass available. ☎ (01726) 842239. Open: 11am–5pm, end of May to end of September. Open for sales all year but telephone to check availability.

The harbour at Mevagissey

Mevagissey Museum

East Quay, Mevagissey
☎ (01726) 843568. Open Easter to October, Weekdays
11am–5pm, Sundays 2pm–5pm.

The coastal path to **Gorran Haven** passes Chapel Point — another place associated with Tristan. He was imprisoned in the chapel but leapt from a window to the safety of a rocky ledge — so the story goes. Views here are reward enough for walkers, even the inland lanes do not compare. Gorran Haven itself is unexpectedly small but opens out into a wide bay.

Dodman Point

This 'noblest of Cornish headlands' is a well preserved Iron Age fort with baulk ditch and rampart. It has been National Trust property since 1919 and this impressive structure can be viewed all round from the circular walk which starts and ends at the Penare car park.

At the extreme point is a huge granite cross, erected in 1896 as a mark for seamen by the Vicar of Caerhays. After dedicating the cross he kept a night's vigil beneath it, praying for the souls of shipwrecked mariners. This same promontory fascinated Sir Arthur Quiller-Couch and he used it in his first book *Dead Man's Rock*. The seas around Dodman Point are the subject of a dispute between the local fishermen and the MOD who want to use it as a firing range.

Hemmick Beach has only a narrow lane beside the water. It is quiet here and there is more than one stretch of sand. Perilous lanes lead to it, so first gear is essential to get to **Porthluney Cove**. There is a large car park here and looking down over the beach, is John Nash's Gothic **Caerhays Castle**, built in 1808 for J.B. Trevanion. A fairytale place, it is scorned by some but loved by all when the rhododendrons are in bloom. When Mr J.C. Williams owned it he cultivated fine rhododendrons, camellias and magnolias. Many species of camellia still bear his name.

Golden Mill

From the Tregony road out of Creed the right-hand turn goes over the Fal to Golden Mill and Manor. This is a privately owned

Caerhays Castle Gardens

Gorran
Open at selected times in spring. Part disabled access. ☎ (01872) 501144 for details.

farm but it is possible to drive as far as the main building without trespassing. The great barn on the left still has the fine windows and sturdy walls of a medieval hall.

A different kind of country house is at **Trewithen**, nearby on the A390. It was the seventeenth-century home of the Hawkins family and 20 acres of its grounds are now internationally famous as Trewithen Gardens, which are open to the public on summer afternoons.

Trewithen Gardens

Grampound Road, near Truro
Privately owned, 20 acres, internationally famous for rare shrubs such as camellias and rhododendrons of special species. Plants for sale on summer afternoons. Teas. Disabled access. ☎ (01726) 882763. Open: 10am–4.30pm Monday to Saturday, March to September.

• APPROACHING ST AUSTELL •

The 'Cornish Alps', bold reminders of Cornwall's china-clay industry, surround St Austell, a pleasant place with old buildings, quietly enjoying the life of a medieval village in the churchtown away from the new shopping precinct and rumbling white clay lorries. Modern interests thrive at the **Arts Centre and Theatre.**

Charlestown harbour

The B3273 leads south to **Pentewan** where stone from Duchy quarries was in great demand for rebuilding churches during the fifteenth century. William Cookworthy's discovery of china clay at Carloggas in the eighteenth century brought new life to this little port. A harbour was built and wagons took their new loads down to waiting ships until tin-streaming soil and china-clay slurry caused the silting which killed it as a port. Today caravans rest on dunes beside the once prosperous harbour. The latter still contains water despite having no access to the sea these days and is well worth going to see.

A footpath goes part of the way to **Black Head** but joins the road where the cliff becomes too sheer for walkers. Views across St Austell Bay to Gribbin Head have a touch of mystery about them for the water shimmers with the constant presence of china clay slurry and the effects are strange and ethereal. Little wonder that Cornwall's famous historian, Dr A.L. Rowse, chose to live at Trenarren on Gerrans Point.

Lost Gardens of Heligan

Before returning to St Austell, no visitor should miss the opportunity of seeing the **Lost Gardens of Heligan** at Pantewan, the largest garden restoration in Britain.

Take the Gorran Haven turning from the B3273 to find this unique collection of gardens within a garden. Formerly the seat of the Tremayne family, the estate had been buried for years under unchecked growth of ivy and bramble, laurels and fallen timber. Now, largely due to the efforts of Tim Smit, it is being revealed and restored in the manner of the great 19th century horticulturists. A minimum of half a day will be needed to explore all the features and stout footwear is advised if a walk around the 'Lost Valley' and the 'Jungle' are to be included.

There are 80 acres of pleasure grounds which include a large collection of rare sub-tropical shrubs, walled gardens, grotto, kitchen garden and ravine fernery. Plant sales. Picnic area. Tea room. Access for the disabled to many areas. Open daily, all year 10am–6pm main season, 10am–5pm in winter. ☎ (01726) 845100.

Charles Rashleigh began to develop the port of **Charlestown,** just outside St Austell, for tin in 1791 and it continued to prosper with the growth of the china clay industry. Then J.T. Treffry of Fowey constructed the port of Par which rivalled both Pentewan and Charlestown, and it is still the main china clay port for smaller vessels. Today the Heritage Centre recreates the heyday of this once thriving port with consummate skill.

The little beach is a pleasant place for fishing, bathing and sailing. Only half a mile along the cliff path is **Carlyon Bay** offering added attractions — the Cornish Leisure World and Polkyth Recreation Centre providing everything from table tennis to opera.

Beside the A390 Ralph Allen was born in a cottage only a few yards along the road towards St Blazey and a small plaque on the wall marks the place. Not many visitors to Cornwall realise that well over a hundred years before Rowland Hill invented the Penny Post, Allen had devised the first real postal system in the country. There is little of architectural interest in this area, but up the hill past Allen's birthplace is the Mid-Cornwall Craft Centre and Galleries at **Biscovey**. First class goods for sale are well displayed and it is also possible to take part in art and craft courses. It is well worth a visit.

Return to the Four Lords and continue down the next hill to **St Blazey**. The church dedicated to St Blaize stands slightly above the Cornish Arms at the bottom of that same hill. St Blaize is not a Cornish saint's name, but in medieval times

Charlestown Shipwreck and Heritage Centre

Quay Road, Charlestown
Exhibitions about local history, shipwrecks and sunken treasure. Artifacts from 1527 and a modern-day audio-visual theatre. Restaurant. Facilities for the disabled. ☎ (01726) 69897.
Open: March to November 10am–5pm daily.

wool was as important as tin in this area and he is the patron saint of wool-combers in the town that was once a port.

Par is its replacement perhaps, the port reclaimed from the sea by Joseph Austen who became Joseph Treffry. His finest achievement was the massive viaduct across the Luxulyan Valley, unbelievably beautiful in bluebell time. A left-hand turn before the St Blazey level crossing, then first right, leads to one of Cornwall's loveliest places, with walks through the woods in plenty. Even the viaduct does not detract from Luxulyan's beauty and standing proud still, though unused, this rail, road and water bridge seems almost part of the woodland scene.

The narrow lane winds to **Luxulyan** village, up and up between stone-littered fields.

Wheal Martyn China Clay Heritage Centre

Carthew
Displays, artifacts, books, pottery and slide programme add to the interest. Picnic areas. Coffee shop. Gift shop. ☎ (01726) 850362. Open: Easter to end of October, 10am–6pm daily.

A short walk guides you past old slurry pits, waterwheels and much else, describing how the clay was obtained for this Cornish industry, which is still important today.

• Annual Events & Festivals •

Throughout West Cornwall there is a busy programme of events and festivals, some ancient and traditional, some of more modern origin but all providing fun and entertainment for visitors and local residents alike. Art exhibitions are held in the various galleries in the region while agricultural shows are a constant feature of the summer calendar, as are flower festivals in spring and summer. Music, drama, literature, sailing, windsurfing, carnivals and air displays, all are catered for. Details can be found in the local press and in the Tourist Information Centres. The following are a few to look out for:

FEBRUARY
- **Hurling**, St Ives and Columb Major Traditional Shrovetide street ball game

MARCH
- **St Piran's Day** (5th)
- **Festival of Spring Gardens** (to end of May)
- **Cornwall County Music Show**, Truro
- **Falmouth Spring Flower Show**

APRIL
- **Trevithick Day**, Camborne

MAY
- **Flora Day**, Helston (8th)
- **Gwennap Feast** Methodist service at Gwennap Pit
- **Daphne du Maurier Festival of Arts and Literature,** Fowey and St Austell

JUNE
- **Three Spires Music Festival**, Truro
- **Golowan Festival**, Penzance
- **Truro Jazz Festival**

JULY
- **RNAS Culdrose Air Day**
- **Camborne Show**

AUGUST
- **Falmouth Carnival**
- **Falmouth Regatta**
- **RAF St Mawgan Air Day**

SEPTEMBER
- **Cornish Gorsedd**, various venues
- **Crying the Neck**, several places
- **St Ives Festival of Music and the Arts**
- **Helston Harvest Fair**
- **Walsingham Pilgrimage** at St Day

OCTOBER
- **Falmouth Oyster Festival**
- **Lowender Peran**, Perranporth Celtic dance and music

DECEMBER
- **Tom Bawcock's Eve**, Mousehole

3

I n Tudor times, the Fal River saw more shipping than any other port in the kingdom and Henry VIII, concerned about possible Spanish attacks, had Pendennis Castle built (English Heritage). It commands Falmouth's best views: on one side, the holiday beaches, on the other, the docks and the town.

In the coaching days, the Green Bank Hotel was important. In the early years of this century, Kenneth Grahame began his *Wind in the Willows* here — proof of this is framed in the lobby. Down High Street — much changed since a disastrous fire in the last century — and to the left, is the Prince of Wales Pier where the Flushing ferry disembarks its passengers. It is also the berth for numerous pleasure boats.

The Moor lies above Market Strand and deceives most people with its name. From the bottom of Jacob's Ladder — 111 steps — boatmen used to ferry people over and moor outside the Seven Stars. This small building (dated 1610) is where generations of innkeepers have drawn beer from the wood, a tradition carried on today.

The granite obelisk in the centre of the Moor is a memorial to men of the Packet Service when 'Falmouth for Orders' was the command obeyed by all captains of these ships. For over 250 years, they carried mail, cargoes and passengers to many parts of the world. In 1833 a wagon loaded with bullion from a packet-ship, left Killigrew Street on Monday and was in London by Saturday.

Falmouth Art Gallery

Municipal Buildings, The Moor, Falmouth
Permanent and temporary exhibitions, shop area, access for disabled. Admission free.
☎ 01326 313863.
Open all year, Monday to Friday 10am–5pm, Saturday 10am–1pm, closed Bank Holidays.

Walking through the town is a casual affair, traffic usually gives priority to pedestrians. In Church Street is the **Falmouth Arts Centre**, where in 1833 the Fox family of Quakers established the Polytechnic Society and reading rooms 'to promote useful arts', setting a trend later followed throughout the country.

At the far end of the town is

SEE PAGE 27 FOR MAP OF THE AREA

Pendennis Castle at Falmouth

the **Georgian Custom House**, handsome with its Greek Doric columns and fine façade. Beside and below, the King's Pipe, a chimney where contraband tobacco was burnt, is an interesting reminder of the manner in which contraband tobacco used to be destroyed.

Off Market Street and clearly sign-posted to Bell's Court is the **Falmouth Maritime Museum**. It is a small but fascinating place housing a variety of items which illustrate Cornwall's maritime history and reflect the truly naval atmosphere of the town itself.

Falmouth Maritime Museum

Bell's Court, Market Street, Falmouth
☎ (01326) 319963.
Open: 10am–5pm daily in summer, 10am–3pm Monday to Saturday in winter.

Opposite Arwenack House is the waterside granite obelisk erected in 1738 by Martin Lister Killigrew as a memorial to his wife's family. They had lived at Arwenack and founded Falmouth, which evolved from Sir Walter Raleigh's plan to develop the harbour. He had stayed at Arwenack with the Killigrews and urged them to press forward with the project. By 1613, in spite of objections from Penryn, the town's identity had been formed and Falmouth was born.

The view over the docks from Castle Drive is one no visitor should miss. With the background of Trefusis Point and the Roseland Peninsula, this busy area is probably unique and there are hopes for a prosperous future as business people appreciate its potential.

Pendennis Castle

Falmouth
Museum, discovery centre, displays of coastal defence armament and access to former secret installations.
☎ (01326) 316594.
Open: 10am–6pm April to September daily, 10am–4pm October to March daily.

Pendennis Castle is a well preserved defence built by Henry VIII in 1539-43, shortly after the Little Dennis blockhouse below it. Later Elizabeth I had it enlarged but it was besieged successfully by Fairfax during the Civil War. Now owned and cared for by English Heritage, its exhibitions and displays are well worth a visit. The old barrack block of the castle is a youth hostel.

Also, ideally situated, at Pendennis Point is the **Maritime Rescue Co-ordination Centre**, opened by Prince Charles in 1981. In 1982 it was the first centre in the eastern Atlantic to answer calls in the Marisat satellite system. Here officials co-ordinate search and rescue round the coastline of Great Britain and Northern Ireland.

The Maritime Rescue Co-ordination Centre

Pendennis Point
Purpose-built coastguard station. Visitors are welcome.
☎ (01326) 314269
(District Controller).

Round the headland, the road leads to Castle Beach, Gyllyngvase and beyond to **Swanpool** and **Maenporth**. These are beautiful beaches with sands and rock pools to keep children happy for the whole holiday. Swanpool — as its name implies — is something else as well; rowing boats and canoes often share the waters with a variety of birds.

Above: Arwenack Street, Falmouth
Below: The Gyllyngvase Gardens at Falmouth

• LEAVING FALMOUTH •

Take the road out of Falmouth which leads past the hospital to Budock, its church and the village of Budock Water. The church was the mother church of Falmouth and had its origins as the centre of a religious community in the sixth century.

The view from Falmouth across to Flushing

An alternative route out of Falmouth leads to **Mabe** with its church high above the Argal and College Reservoirs. Look down from the Penryn-Constantine road (B3291) and pause to walk or fish.

The way to **Mawnan Smith** passes **Penjerrick Gardens**, a Fox property now open to the public. The Fox family created this garden where famous Cornish rhododendrons were raised. Springtime is best for a visit here — then the flowering shrubs are a mass of colour and one of the largest magnolias in existence can be seen.

Penjerrick Gardens

1 mile S of Budock Vean
☎ (01326) 870105.
Open: March to September.

From the beaches, the coast path goes to **Rosemullion Head** but motorists are restricted to the road which ends at Mawnan church. It was built on an Iron Age site, the tower warning seamen that they were near the dreaded Manacle Rocks. Over the lych-gate an inscription in Cornish reads: *Da thym ythyn nesse the Thu* which means 'It is good for me to draw nigh unto the Lord'. Inside is a wide variety of colourful tapestry kneelers, those of the choir are patterned with medieval tunes.

Round the headland lies **Durgan**, a tiny village reached either by cliff path or road by way of Mawnan Smith. It consists of a handful of cottages, just beside the small beach. There is no sand here, but safe bathing and an ideal place for windsurfing. This area, together with Glendurgan, is National Trust property. Although the house is occupied by members of the Fox family and is not open to the public, the valley garden may be visited. It is a garden of great beauty with fine trees and shrubs, walled and water gardens; a wooded valley runs down to Durgan on the Helford River.

Nearby is another place of delight beside the Helford River. **Trebah Gardens** is dramatic, uniquely beautiful and a friendly paradise for children and families. Dogs are allowed provided they are kept on their leads.

Trebah Gardens

Mawnan Smith, Falmouth
☎ (01326) 250448.
Open 10.30am–5pm, all year.

Mylor Bridge, north of Falmouth, is at the head of the creek though the original settlement was the churchtown at its mouth a mile away. In the mid-nineteenth century the buildings by the pier were known as *HMS Ganges*, at that time the Royal Navy's only shore-based training centre and hospital. The ship, however, was anchored at St Just Pool across the Carrick Roads.

Glendurgan Gardens

Best seen in spring for flowering shrubs especially magnolias and camellias; laurel maze, viewpoint on Manderson's Hill.
☎ (01326) 250906.
Open: 10.30am–5.30pm. Open from March until October. Closed on Sundays and Mondays, Good Friday.

Today it is a yachting centre but the restaurant there still bears the old name.

The walk ends at **Flushing**, meeting the road from Mylor. Its Celtic name was Nankersey, but when Dutch engineers arrived to build Falmouth's quays, they settled here and changed the name as a reminder of their homeland. The cottages cling to the waterside, the village is reputed to have the mildest climate in the country and flowers bloom here all the year round as if endorsing that claim.

St Mylor Church

Almost hidden in trees, beside the water, stands **St Mylor church**. It is a picturesque building with a separate bell tower and Cornwall's tallest cross embedded in the ground at the south door. One of the epitaphs is unusaual and visitors are always told to read about Joseph Crapp, a shipwright who died 'ye 26th of November 1770, aged 43 years.' His death is graphically described:

Alas friend Joseph
His end was almost sudden
As thugh a mandate came
Express from heaven
His foot, it slip and he did fall
Help, help he cries,
and that was all

One gravestone is 'To the Memory of the Warriors, Women and Children, who on their return to England from the coast of Spain; unhappily perished in the Wreck of the *Queen Transport*, on Trefusis Point, Jany 14, 1814', just one of the many ships wrecked off the Cornish coast. Inside, the carved wood of the pulpit is believed to have come from Armada wrecks but the choir screen recalls more recent events. It was given in memory of those drowned in 1966 when an overloaded local pleasure boat capsized.

• PENRYN •

At the head of the river is Penryn, reached either by a waterside path or inland road. These ways meet at the bottom of the steep hill beside St Gluvias, the parish church of Penryn. A place to visit is the Town Hall Museum. It was once the gaol but now houses a variety of interesting items connected with Penryn's history.

Penryn Museum

Stands centrally on Penryn's spine road
☎ (01326) 372158.
Open all year, Monday to Friday, 10am–4pm.
Opening times may vary as staffed by volunteers.
Check with Town Hall ☎ (01326) 373086.

The town, in fact, grew from a settlement on the hill across the river. It has an interesting history, part splendid, part sad, but cherishes hopes for the future.

Founded as a borough in 1216, it was granted a charter in 1236 and saw the rise and fall of Glasney collegiate church from 1265 to 1549. This establishment was a centre for religious instruction (renowned throughout Europe), growing in importance as Penryn's trade increased.

The closure of Glasney at the Dissolution, however, followed by the unexpected rise of Falmouth at the mouth of the river, led to a decline from which Penryn has never really recovered.

However, in 1977 its unique medieval character was recognised as rare, and Government grants were given to save old buildings, so bringing a conservation programme into being. As a result, the town whose granite is to be seen in buildings as different as London's Thames Embankment, Singapore harbour and Fastnet Lighthouse, is fast becoming a tourist attraction.

The Goonhilly Earth Station

• HELSTON & AROUND •

About halfway between Truro and Penzance is historic Helston, a town apparently oblivious of the A394 traffic which divides it. But on 8 May each year, the past takes over as old houses and twisting streets echo with Flora Day celebrations — once a pagan welcome to spring.

The Angel Hotel is an attractive building with parts dating from the sixteenth century. At the end of the seventeenth century it was the town house of Cornwall's great statesman, Sidney Godolphin and later it became the Excise House. This included the Assembly Rooms with a minstrels' gallery.

The Blue Anchor Inn is another ancient pub which has brewed its own beer for centuries.

Helston's 1305 charter ruled that tinners should bring their mineral here for coinage or testing. Below the old Grammar School where Charles Kingsley was educated, Coinagehall Street is an echo of medieval days. In 1576 a market house was built here and it incorporated the Town Hall. The classical structure of the **Guildhall** seen today, when erected in 1837–8 also had a corn market in part of the building, so carrying on the purpose of the original.

The church is at the back of the town beyond the **Museum** but the latter should not be missed, particularly with its emphasis on

The Blue Anchor Inn, Helston

the former crafts and industries which flourished in and around Helston during the nineteenth and early twentieth centuries. It has a good display of folk history which includes Henry Trengrouse's life-saving rocket — invented after the Anson shipwreck on Loe Bar. Modern crafts are on display at Crefton, across the road: open most days.

The Lizard & Helston

Map labels:
B3297, B3303, Carnkie, A394, A39, FALMOUTH, Pendennis Castle, Poldark Mine Heritage Complex, Trevarno Manor Garden, Sithney, Breage, Penjerrick Gardens, HELSTON, Flambards, Gweek, Trebah Gardens, Port Navas, Mawnan Smith, Glendurgan Garden, Culdrose Viewing Centre, Durgan, St Anthony, B3304, Loe Pool, Porthleven, Helford, Mawgan, Manaccan, Trelowarren House, A3083, Porthoustock, St Keverne, Goonhilly Earth Station, B3293, Gunwalloe, Poldhu, Mullion, Coverack, Mullion Cove, Black Head, St Ruan, Cadgwith, Grade, Kynance Cove, Lizard, Lizard Point

★ Angel Hotel
★ Butter Market Museum
★ Guildhall

0   4 miles
0   6 Km

Butter Market Museum

In the former Market House in Church Street. It was built in 1837–8 and was composed of two buildings, one selling butter and eggs, the other meat. ☎ (01326) 564027. Open: 10.30am–1pm and 2pm–4.30pm all week except Wednesday when it closes at 12noon. Closed Sundays and Bank Holidays.

Fresh fish and craft shops in Meneage Street are of above average quality, as is Monday's cattle market at the lower end of the town.

The B3304 passes the boating pool on the Porthleven Road but walkers and ornithologists will want to explore the grounds of seventeenth-century Penrose beside **Loe Pool**, Cornwall's largest lake. This freshwater lake is an unusual example of the 'drowned valleys' occurring in Devon and Cornwall. The Loe Bar formed by accumulated shingle from the Atlantic has dammed the former estuary which made the port of Helston.

Loe Pool, owned by the Rogers family since 1770, is the main feature of their gift to the National Trust in 1974 — some 1,600 acres altogether, the largest from Cornwall. A condition of this gift, that it be kept as a place of quiet beauty, makes it excellent for bird-watching. The house itself is not open. There is easy parking at the two entrances and the 6-mile walk taking in Loe Bar Sands will probably mean a rambling day and a picnic. The Loe is a long shingle bank dividing the freshwater lake from the sea.

Porthleven is the birthplace of Guy Gibson, 'Dambusters' hero, and a road bears his name. It is a good place for tea after wandering through its narrow streets and visiting Breageside by the harbour. This was once the heart of a thriving port — note the picturesque store built originally to hold some 7,000 tons of china clay.

Off the A394 to Penzance, running almost parallel with the coast, several lanes lead to headlands and byways. **Trewavas Head** (Joseph Trewavas received Cornwall's first VC in 1856) and nearby **Rinsey Head** are ideal for picnics. Part of the area and the car park belong to the National Trust, who have partly restored the engine house and chimney of a disused copper mine, Wheal Prosper.

There are footpaths only for **Cudden Point** with its unusual view of St Michael's Mount. Walkers will enjoy Prussia Cove and Betsy's Cove, both haunts of John Carter, eighteenth-century smuggler and self-styled 'King of Prussia'.

The great inland mining area is reached via **Goldsithney**, a busy place in coaching days, now a quiet village. The main building of St Hilary church dates from 1854 but the tower dates from the thirteenth century, while an inscribed stone in the churchyard is probably sixth century.

Off the B3280, a turn to the village of **Godolphin Cross** comes after the hamlets of Relubbus and Bosence, both busy, lively places in Roman times. Relubbus had the tide at its feet and Roman remains at Bosence prove its trading capabilities. Deep in woodland lies Godolphin, a house which deserves a book to itself. This fifteenth-century mansion was built with wealth from nearby mines. Sir Sidney Godolphin, Elizabeth I's great High Treasurer, and the famed Godolphin Arab stallion are only part of the history associated with this property.

Godolphin House

Breage
Fifteenth-century mansion, standing 3 miles from Mounts Bay on the lower slopes of Godolphin Hill. Tin mines provided the family fortune.
☎ (01736) 762409.
Open: 2pm–5pm May and June, Thursday; 2pm–5pm July and September, Tuesday and Thursday; 10am–1pm August, Thursday.

The whole area of Godolphin and Tregonning is ideal for walks and picnics are made more pleasant by easy roadside parking.

• THE LIZARD PENINSULA •

From Helston, the Lizard Peninsula can be explored by turning off the A394 Falmouth road past Trewennack to Gweek. Pleasant high-hedged lanes lead to Boskenwyn Downs and open on to a straight road probably constructed by the Romans to take tin from Grumbla to the port. Gweek's unusual name comes from the Latin Vicus which confirms the Roman presence.

Kynance Cove

Since very early times the valleys all round have been streamed for tin, and careful observers may still discover ancient tin moulds built into the quay walls. In 1201 Gweek was important enough to warrant a merchant guild as well as burgess privileges.

The creek is now silted up but beside it is the **Cornish Seal Sanctuary**, the Marine Animal Rescue Centre. It was established in the late 1950s and is the largest in Europe. Over the years the objectives of this conservation centre have been expanded and it now cares for all marine animals. It also shows how everyone can help.

Cornish Seal Sanctuary

Gweek
Devoted to seal rescue and care. Baby seals are in the hospital from September to March, but others are always on view. Two safari trains are available for transport from the car park to the main points beside the lovely Gweek River.
☎ (01326) 221874.
Open: 9am–5pm daily except Christmas Day.

The B3292 to St Keverne runs between a thatched tollhouse and the water — a pretty road affording occasional glimpses of the creek and walks through the woods. But a narrower primrose-clad lane on the far side of the house offers rewards for brave motorists. It is narrow and steep, winding up past an ancient earthwork, dipping through beech and elm woods before crossing the B3293 to wander up and down into the valley where **Mawgan-in-Meneage** lies.

The whole parish of Monks (Meneage or Menaig seems to come from Cornish managh or monk) is full of beauty and history — its church provides something of both. Look for the seventeenth-century sundial, a dog door and an unusual brass memorial to the unknown Hannibal Basset with the words 'Shall we all die'.

Frenchman's Creek

Keep to the Manaccan road through wooded lanes until a signpost to Kestle is reached. This lane leads to the unbelievably beautiful haven of **Frenchman's Creek**, which Daphne du Maurier saw, loved and made famous in her book of the same name. It has rightly been described as a place of 'distinct, eerie charm' and access to it is close by the farm. Over 35 acres along the south bank are National Trust property and footpaths go to Tremayne Quay and Helford.

Motorists should return to the Manaccan road for **Helford** to see its thatched beauty, stop at the old Shipwrights' Arms and cross the river at Monks' Passage to the Ferryboat Inn.

The memorial at St Kaverne to the victims of the SS Mohegan which went down on the Manacles Reef

St Anthony church on the beach at **Gillan** harbour is as beautiful as its surroundings. This was a busy port in medieval times, with ships sailing to Southampton loaded with fish, fish oil, hides, slate and tin. Today, the charm of this quiet corner of the Lizard lies in its remoteness and not in trade.

The lonely village across the water is protected by a difficult access road so walkers may follow the coastal path, as motorists have to turn inland again. The wild cliffs and fierce rocks explain the need for a coastguard and the lifeboat that was stationed here from 1869–1945, rescuing ships from the dreaded Manacles. **Porthoustock** (P'roustock) is a somewhat calmer place today as local men find quarrying roadstone safer than fishing.

St Keverne church has reminders of ships wrecked on the dreaded Manacles and has rightly been called the 'church of heartbreak'. A plaque on the churchyard wall is in memory of Michael Josef an Gof, the blacksmith who led the Cornish army to Blackheath with Thomas Flamank of Bodmin. This was the first rebellion of 1497 and he paid for this fight with his life. However, before his grim death at London's Tyburn, he told the crowd that both his name and fame would not be forgotten. His words came true for his memory and deed lives still in the hearts of all Cornishmen.

The road to **Manaccan** is a delight. So is the village, perched saucily on a hillside. Geologists will remember that William Gregor discovered titanium from here and all should note that ill luck befalls those who pick figs from the tree in the church wall. Few, however, may know that Bligh of the Bounty came here to survey for the Admiralty, was mistaken for a French spy and promptly arrested. The centuries-old New Inn provides a wide variety of good food — beside a log fire.

At this point some may wish to return to Helston, wandering quietly through the narrow lanes. If so, look for **Trelowarren**, between the villages of St Martin's and Garras.

Trelowarren House and Craft Centre

Mawgan-in-Meneage
Elizabethan-style Stuart building with a Victorian interior.
Crafts exhibition (July and August), book shop, craft shop,
coffee bar, woodland walks. ☎ (01326) 221224.
Open: Easter to end of September, 11am–5pm.

Probably first owned by Earl Harold before Domesday, Trelwowarren has been the home of the Vyvyan family since 1426 and the handsome house is now used for conferences and retreats. One of the most secluded caravan parks in Cornwall takes a small part of the extensive grounds, and a cluster of former barns and outhouses have their own attractions. A small pottery and an excellent restaurant will tempt most people while others may like to buy Trelowarren herb plants or visit one of the variety of craft exhibitions held throughout the summer. **The Lizard Countryside Centre** also offers local information in a variety of ways.

Lizard Countryside Centre

Trelowarren Estate
Interpretation of countryside, farming, history, wildlife. Gift shop.
☎ (01326) 221661.
Open: 11am–5pm daily.

Coverack harbour

There is even more to see and enjoy on the western side of the Lizard so allow plenty of time for this. Immediately outside Helston is the **Royal Naval Air Station at Culdrose.** It is Europe's largest helicopter base and has recently celebrated its 40th birthday, marking the date by enlarging its public viewing area.

A very different kind of entertainment is to be found just off that same road in the **Cornwall Aero Park and Flambards Victorian Village.** All-weather family amusements are set out here and include a life-size layout model of the London blitz and a Victorian village with life-size reconstructions.

The B3293 from here will lead you to **Goon-hilly Downs** and the startling sight of a group of futuristic-looking dishes. This is the **Goonhilly Earth Station,** now British Telecom International, where the enormous aerials turn to the sky like creatures of science fiction. They were sited in this particular area because only the depth of granite found here was strong enough to bear the weight of these impressive structures.

July 1987 saw the first quarter century of these satellite communications. There is a very fine centre for visitors. Here you can study working models of both dishes and satellites and enjoy the well presented audio-visual explanation of the mystery of modern telecommunications. There is also a restaurant of first-class quality.

Royal Naval Air Station

Culdrose
This is beside the A3083 Helston-Lizard road. It is one of Europe's largest stations and machines are always on standby. Public viewing enclosure is close to the B3291. Gift shop and café.

Cornwall Aero Park and Flambards Victorian Village

Helston
Theme park with exciting rides, exhibitions, aeroplanes, helicopter flights in high season.
☎ (01326) 564093.
Open: 10am–5pm April to November on most days.

Goonhilly Earth Station

Beside the B3293
There is a public viewing enclosure and visitor centre.
☎ (0800) 679593.
Open: 10am–6pm Easter to end of October daily.

Above: Whiling away the hours at Mullion Harbour
Below: Mullion Harbour at low tide

From July to October the barren downs which surround the Earth Station are brilliant with white-pink and deep lilac Cornish heather which is rarely found anywhere else in Britain. A walk round the adjoining National Nature Reserve affords the chance to see some of the Lizard's unique flora.

About 4 miles farther along the B3294 is **Coverack,** a picturesque village, still mainly Cornish in character, with an appeal for those who enjoy sea views and a safe beach. The local lifeboat station is a particular place of interest.

There are numerous cliff walks in this area, the one leading to **Kennack Sands** ends in a safe beach for swimming in fine weather.

The motorist, however, must return to the B3293 and turn left at Traboe Cross in order to reach the National Trust **Poltesco Cove.** It is reached by scrambling down beside a trout stream, but is well worth the effort, and for energetic walkers, there are nature trails to follow.

Serpentine

Cadgwith is a very 'picture-postcard' village which is a little sad because it has lost most of its former fishing activities, although it still attracts artists and photographers. Serpentine can be found around these parts, and inland from Cadgwith, great blocks of it can be seen in the church towers of St Ruan and Grade — the latter to be found at the end of a cart track.

All the cliff walks round here offer spectacular views. At **Lizard Point** the motorist has to go inland a short way from Landewednack and Grade to reach **Lizard village** which is little more than a cluster of souvenir shops with serpentine goods in great variety. At the end of the road is a lifeboat station and also Britain's most southerly beacon with interesting historical points to note. It was from here, about 400 years ago, in the summer of 1588, that the ships of the Spanish Armada were first sighted.

In the mid-eighteenth century, two towers were built here to house a coal-fired warning light, but that produced so many problems that the idea was abandoned until oil lamps were installed in 1812. 1840 saw the first fog signals, and in 1878, a steam-driven generator powered two electric arc lamps which gave good service until 1903 when they were replaced by a single 12 million candlepower beam. The light that shines from the Lizard today is

Lizard Lighthouse

Built in 1751. Squat building with white walls, cowls and fog-horns. ☎ (01326) 290431.

one of the most powerful in the world, even though in 1926 its brilliance was reduced because local fishermen claimed the brightness ruined the pilchard fishing.

Cliff walkers will have no problem in finding the lovely places along the western coast of the Lizard Peninsula — **Kynance, Mullion** and **Gunwalloe** — before the return to Helston. Perhaps this is one of Cornwall's finest cliff walks because, not only are there attractive villages to see en route, but all the time there is a view of St Michael's Mount, topped by its fairytale castle and looking different at every turn.

Motorists will need to watch for signpost directions along the Lizard-Helston A3083, watching particularly for the turn to Cury and Poldhu. On the cliffs of **Poldhu Cove** is Guglielmo Marconi's

memorial, a granite column, now the only reminder of the momentous events which took place on these high cliffs overlooking Mount's Bay, for the historic buildings were dismantled in 1937.

Marconi Memorial

Poldhu
Spot marked by a small obelisk on the golf course.

In 1900, Marconi chose to erect a wireless station, of a size never before believed possible, on this site. Then, on 12 December 1901, Poldhu was revealed as the cradle of the radio age when signals sent from here bridged the Atlantic and were received by Marconi at St John, Newfoundland. So wireless telegraphy was born here and, in time, played a vital part in World War I.

Later, in 1924, the Marconi-Franklin beam system was also transmitted from here and revolutionised long-range radio communication. Short-wave beam systems followed and it is also interesting to note that the coaxial cable, which is an integral feature of every home television installation, was devised in the course of research done at Poldhu.

So, although the Lizard Peninsula may seem small in relation to the rest of Cornwall, it has been, and will continue to be, responsible for events that make vital contributions to the progress of world science. A thought to remember on the return to Helston.

The rotating optical faces of the Lizard light create a beam that has a range of 26 miles from a 400-watt bulb

5
Penzance and West Penwith

Rail travellers have always thought of Penzance as the place of journey's end. It is certainly the rail terminus in the west but the locals say that it is in fact where Cornwall begins. Before exploring the area of West Penwith (*Penwyth* is the Cornish for extremity) to discover the truth of this statement, there is much to enjoy in the town of Penzance itself, for it is a place of surprises.

• PENZANCE •

Beautiful still, with its high, stone-stepped pavement is Market Jew Street, the main thoroughfare which greets pedestrians, motorists and rail travellers who have left the station at the bottom of the hill. The long road leads to the handsome granite Town Hall, before which stands the statue of Sir Humphry Davy.

He was born in a house close by and there, too, began the experiments which eventually brought him fame. He was knighted in 1812 for his contributions to science and was later created baronet for his invention of the miner's safety lamp.

The road behind the former town hall, now the Market Hall, turns left towards the harbour and the Barbican Aquarium down Chapel Street. This once bustled with mule trains laden with their copper ore for ships' cargoes. Now it is a backwater of memories, many of them lingering in the Union Hotel where the Battle of Trafalgar victory was first announced from the minstrel's gallery. Local fishermen had learnt it from the ship racing up-channel to Falmouth with the news.

Such was local pride in this 'first' that Penzance men made the Nelson banner (now in Madron church) which has ever since been carried in procession on the Sunday nearest to Trafalgar Day. At the back of this historic building there is the shell of a Georgian theatre, opened in 1789: restoration work has begun. Here miners sought relaxation in the performances of Edmund Keen, Grossmith and other well known actors.

At the Youth Hostel at Castle Horneck is a tree planted to celebrate the Battle of Trafalgar in 1805.

Porthcurno beach

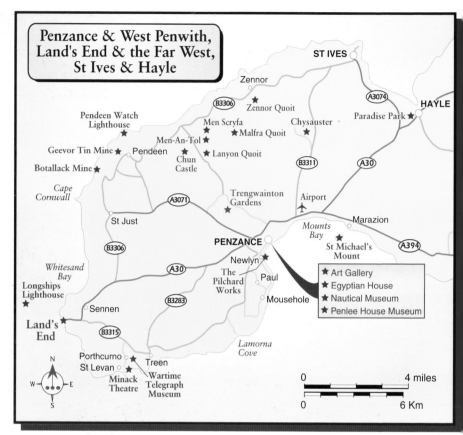

Penzance & West Penwith, Land's End & the Far West, St Ives & Hayle

ST IVES

Zennor
B3306
Zennor Quoit

Pendeen Watch Lighthouse
Men Scryfa
★ Malfra Quoit
Chysauster
Paradise Park ★
HAYLE
A3074

Men-An-Tol ★
Geevor Tin Mine ★ Pendeen
★ Lanyon Quoit
Chun Castle
B3311
A30

Botallack Mine ★

Cape Cornwall

A3071
Trengwainton Gardens
Airport
Marazion

St Just
Mounts Bay
St Michael's Mount
A394

B3306
PENZANCE

Whitesand Bay
A30
Newlyn
The Pilchard Works
Paul
★ Art Gallery
★ Egyptian House
★ Nautical Museum
★ Penlee House Museum

Longships Lighthouse
B3283
Mousehole

Sennen

Land's End
B3315

Lamorna Cove

N
Porthcurno
St Levan
Treen
Minack Theatre
Wartime Telegraph Museum

0 ——— 4 miles
0 ——— 6 Km

Number 25 Chapel Street claims different honours. It was the home of Maria Branwell who married in Yorkshire and became mother to Charlotte, Emily, Anne and Branwell Brontë. She never lost her love for Cornwall, remembering it even on her death bed when she begged the nurse to raise her up so that she could watch her clear the grate because 'she did it as it was done in Cornwall.' The house is not open to the public.

The National Trust's **Egyptian House** with its flamboyant façade, also in Chapel Street, is of unusual interest. Restored by the Landmark Trust, part of the ground floor is now taken up by a National Trust shop. The Admiral Benbow Restaurant and **Maritime Museum** are at the sea end of this old-fashioned street and are also worth a visit.

Maritime Museum

Chapel Street

Varied, interesting, appropriate exhibits for this maritime place, with many items recovered by divers investigating historic wrecks. ☎ (01736) 368890. Open: 10.30am–4.30pm, Monday to Saturday from Easter to end of October.

There are many side ways and shop-lined lanes to explore in this most western of Cornish towns. Each has something to offer, but beyond Market Jew Street, the road leads on to Alverton, with St John's Hall whose handsome granite facade houses the Town Clerk's office.

Cornwall Geological Museum

St John's Hall

One of the finest geological displays in Europe revealing geological secrets of the planet and displaying West Cornwall's mineral importance.

☎ (01736) 332400.

☎ (01736) 330183 for opening times and group bookings.

The Egyptian House, Penzance, now a National Trust shop

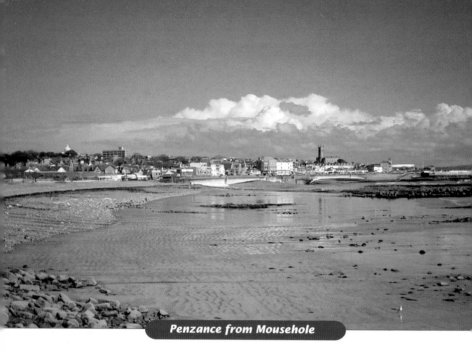

Penzance from Mousehole

Not far away is the **Penlee House Museum** — a place of many treasures standing in subtropical gardens where camellias bloom at Christmas above the long promenade stretching from Newlyn to the memorial at the end of Chapel Street.

If you are a walker, telephone (01736) 369409 for details of guided walks round the Penwith beyond Penzance. Before moving on from Penzance itself a visit to the **Trinity House National Lighthouse Centre** will prove entertaining and enlightening about the working conditions of lighthouse keepers.

Penlee House Art Gallery and Museum

Morrab Road, Penzance
Entirely local display reflecting the history and environment of Penzance. Unrivalled collection of work by the Victorian Newlyn School of Painting. Wheel-chair access, gift shop, café. ☎ (01736) 363625. Open Monday to Saturday 10.30am– 4.30pm, also Sundays in July and August 12pm–4.30pm.

Trinity House National Lighthouse Centre

Hands-on museum, audio-visual display, reconstructed living quarters of a lighthouse keeper. ☎ (01736) 360077.
Open: 10.30am–4.30pm, Easter to end of October, daily.

• WEST PENWITH •

From here, the road follows the vast, magnificent sweep of Mount's Bay past the Heliport (for the Isles of Scilly) and Long Rock to Marazion. This place is a delight, with its view of St Michael's Mount (acknowledged to be the earliest identifiable place in Britain). Its golden sands and safe bathing are ideal for children while the marshes nearby attract birdwatchers. Marazion was a thriving port as long ago as the Bronze Age as it was on one of the main overland routes for merchants taking Irish gold to Brittany.

St Michael's Mount from Mount's bay

Ordnance Survey maps mark **Long Rock** just offshore and the houses along the main road take their name from it.

Legend relates that St Michael appeared to some hermits, supposedly on a large rock, which has ever since been known as St Michael's Chair, while history tells us that it was Edward the Confessor who established a Benedictine chapel on **St Michael's Mount**. The monks' domestic buildings are now incorporated in the fourteenth-century castle on the rock summit but the abbot's kitchen is well preserved and stands apart.

Even grey skies cannot dim the magical quality of the Mount, which was given by Lord St Levan to the National Trust in 1954. His son, the fourth baron, now lives here. Visitors reach it by foot across a causeway or ferry from Marazion. Apart from the situation of this spectacular retreat with its fine views towards Land's End and the Lizard across Mount's Bay, there is interest here for all. The harbour and village may always be visited, but visitors should check for opening days of the castle beforehand.

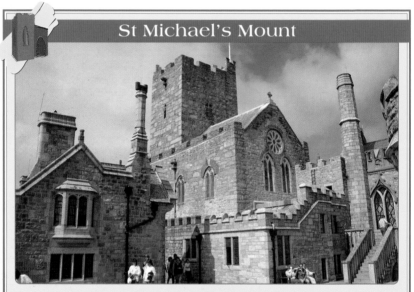

St Michael's Mount

When the approach causeway is covered there is a ferry service from Marazion. Owing to the quick tidal movement visitors will probably walk back so return tickets should not be taken. The small chapel is unusual in size and location. It is open on Sunday at 10.30 for Divine Service which begins at 11am. Café and National Trust shop. Some guided tours in winter months. Telephone for details, ☎ (01736) 710265. Mount and Castle open April to end of October, Monday to Friday 10.30am–5.30pm, the Mount is open most weekends in summer.

In any case it would be easy to spend a whole day here thinking of the past: perhaps of 1497 when Perkin Warbeck left his wife on the Mount to make an abortive claim for England's throne, or of 1549 when the owners of the castle were involved in the Prayer Book Rebellion, or possibly even of 1642–3 when the future King Charles II was given sanctuary en route for the Isles of Scilly — a plaque proclaiming this is on the wall of a house in Marazion.

In 1981, an unusual scheme was proposed by Lord St Levan. He decided to reconstruct a twelfth-century monastic herb garden.

His idea was to grow medicinal plants used by the Benedictines, especially those for the relief of toothache as they were much sought after by pilgrims.

From the steep B3309 below the church towards Crowlas, the second lane on the left leads to the exciting Penwith countryside, studied by Borlase. A lane curves round the foot of **Trencrom Hill,** part of the granite backbone of West Penwith — a site that was given to the National Trust by Colonel G.L. Tyringham of Lelant in memory of the men and women in Cornwall who gave their lives in the two World Wars. Between St Michael's Mount and St Ives, it consists of 64 acres of gorse-covered hill ideal for walks and picnics, overlooking fine views of both land and sea. The soil here is good and Channel Island herds thrive in the area.

The way to **Castle-an-Dinas** and **Chysauster** is down the Nancledra valley where tin has been streamed since earliest times. The former is one of the chain of hill forts across the country, the latter (along a pleasant lane off the B3311) probably one of the best preserved beehive hut circles in Great Britain. It was an Iron Age village from about the second century BC to the third century AD and consists now of a series of stone houses, each containing a number of rooms. Partial excavations have been made here and the walls of the buildings are still clearly visible.

Chysauster

2.5 miles NW of Gulval (English Heritage)
An Iron Age village, it consists of a series of stone houses, each containing a number of rooms. Parking and toilet facilities.
☎ (0831) 757934. Open daily 10am–6pm, April to October.

Not far away at the head of the Trevaylor valley, towering over the Penwith Peninsula is **Mulfra Quoit.** This close group of standing stones on the site of an ancient settlement at Mulfra Hill, gives substantial evidence to the theory of ancient ley lines. Three of the four original uprights still stand and support a partially displaced capstone. Traces of a circular barrow about 40ft in diameter can be seen, the original covering of the chamber.

Also in the same area is the **Men-an-Tol**, a fascinating monument with numerous legends. In 1749 Dr Borlase learnt that local people still crept through the hole to cure their rheumatism, while children who suffered from rickets were passed through it at certain times of the year. Sir Norman Lockyer wrote that this megalith was an astronomical instrument for the observation of certain sunrises and sunsets.

Close by are the **Men Scryfa** (Inscribed Stone) and the **Nine Maidens Stone Circle**. Were these stones really girls who had danced on the Sabbath and had been turned to stone for their sin? That is what the legend says.

The Men Scryfa, however, is thought to be closer to reality — some think it was the grave of a giant warrior, others consider it another ley marker and there are those who think it could be the gravestone of the noble Rialobran (Royal Raven) who lived between the fifth and sixth centuries BC on nearby Carn Galver.

Men Scryfa

3 miles NW of Madron.
Up a side lane beside the Morvah–Madron road is an 8ft tall inscribed stone. *Rialobranus Cunovali Fili* is the Roman inscription and could be translated as 'Son of Chief Royal Raven'.

Beside the lonely secondary road which runs from Morvah to Madron stands **Lanyon Quoit** — probably Cornwall's most famous monument and the only known example of the remains of a long barrow. It was originally 90ft long and its capstone so high that Dr Borlase rode his horse under it. Storm damage accounts for the present lower height. It was re-erected by public subscription in 1824 after a violent storm (1815) broke one of its four stone supports. The ruined engine house on the ridge behind is at the Ding Dong Mine.

Madron village is where this road joins the B3312 into Penzance. It is high over the port and has a huddle of cottages pleasantly grouped near the church which is named after a sixth-century holy man from Brittany, Maddern. It is the mother church of Penzance and, acknowledged to be one of Cornwall's finest, is well worth a visit. The pew ends are unusually fine, there is the Nelson banner (mentioned earlier) and the great bell from the famous Ding-Dong Mine, whose ruined engine house is silhouetted starkly on the high land ridge behind the village.

Tregiffan burial mound at the roadside with the Merry Maidens stone circle nearby

Lanyon Quoit

4 miles NW of Penzance, via B3312

A huge granite capstone (18ft x 9ft) on three upright stones, the most famous of Cornish antiquities as well as the most restored.

A short distance away is Madron's famous wishing well, the water from which is said to have effected many miracle cures. Those who care to walk about half a mile down a damp ferny lane will probably see rags hanging from the surrounding bushes —offerings still made to St Maddern, possibly for happiness in love or simply to placate the invisible spirits and hope for their protection. Here there is also the restored fourteenth-century baptistry of St Madron.

The lovely **Trengwainton Gardens**, a National Trust property, lies beside the A3071 below Madron. There has been a house here since the sixteenth century, but it is now privately owned. In 1814, Rose Price, the son of a rich West Indian sugar planter, bought the house and estate and began to develop it along the lines seen today. He enlarged the original house, gave it a granite façade, built the lodge, planned the walled gardens and planted the magnificent woods of beech and sycamore which are so greatly admired today.

The 98 acres of park and garden were given to the National Trust in 1961 by Lieutenant Colonel Sir Edward Bolitho. It is interesting to learn that today's beauty has been created mainly over the last 40 years with help from three great Cornish gardeners — Mr J.C. Williams of Caerhays, Mr P.D. Williams of Lanarth and Canon Boscawen of Ludgvan. The walled gardens contain many tender plants, which cannot be grown in the open anywhere else in Britain, thanks to the proximity of the Gulf Stream which affords almost completely frost-free gardening here.

Trengwainton Gardens

A3071

Rare plants from Burma and Assam. A garden of exotic delight, probably at its best in springtime. Shop and tea room.
☎ (01736) 362297.
Open March–October, Sunday to Thursday (and Good Friday) 10.00am–5.30pm (5pm in March and October).

Mousehole harbour

Fishing is still very much part of the life of **Newlyn** as can be seen by visiting the **Pilchard Works** just upstream of Newlyn bridge. This unique, award winning, heritage museum is part of the last salt processing pilchard factory in the country where the fish are still packed in wooden boxes and casks for export. Visitors can see the working pilchard presses, learn about the history of the industry and view examples of Newlyn's 19th-century Arts and Crafts Movement.

The name Penlee reverberated round the land, like the tolling of a funeral bell, at the end of 1981 when storms off this coast caused a lifeboat tragedy. **Penlee Point** is on the coast road to **Mousehole** (Mouzel), the prettiest fishing village according to many visitors, and which, with Penzance and Newlyn, was burned by the

Pilchard Works

Newlyn

Factory with heritage museum, local history displays, examples of Newlyn copper. ☎ (01736) 332112.
Open: 10am–6pm Monday to Friday, 10am–4pm Saturday, Easter to October.

Lamorna valley

Only 2 miles along the cliff path, but further by road past the Roman encampment of Castallack, lies the fertile and lovely **Lamorna valley**. A bubbling trout stream and colourful gardens tempt visitors down to the little harbour or cove, justly known as one of Cornwall's loveliest, enticing them to linger. The artist Samuel John Birch could not leave, added Lamorna to his name, and gained fame as S.J. Lamorna Birch RA.

The 10-mile cliff walk from here to Land's End is one that should not be hurried. There are flowers, birds and views sufficient to satisfy everyone, but few people know the story of how the famous Marconi met and fell in love with Betty Paynter on the Lamorna cliffs. She was then the fifteen-year-old daughter of Colonel Paynter of nearby Boskenna House, but the vast difference in age did not stop the engineer. He installed a radio receiver in her schoolroom at home, sent diamond bracelets to her at school and sailed his yacht into Bournemouth almost every weekend in the hope of a meeting.

A story in the best romantic tradition, but one that did not end according to the Cinderella pattern. After 3 years of fun and friendship, the schoolgirl, then grown up, realised that the love was all on his side and refused him for the last time.

Lamorna Cove

Spaniards in July 1595 and almost destroyed. Its delightful cluster of cottages hugging the harbour appeals to artists, photographers and most holidaymakers.

Above Lamorna Cove, past Trewoofe (Troove) is **Boleigh**, site of the last battle between the Cornish and the English, which took place in AD935. To celebrate his victory, King Athelstan gave a charter to found a collegiate church at **St Buryan**. The two immense megaliths known as 'the Pipers' are believed to have been erected by the king as peace stones to seal the treaty.

On the other side of the road is another group of stones — the **Merry Maidens**. It consists of nineteen stones, is about 75ft in diameter and is one of the places where the Cornish Gorsedd is sometimes held. This gathering is an annual event at which new bards are admitted to the Gorsedd, or College of Bards, an organisation unique to Celtic communities enshrining their common cultural heritage.

St Buryan is a handsome church of the late fifteenth century with a fine rood screen and a 92ft granite tower. Further along the B3283 lies the village of **Treen**, once the heart of a busy tin-streaming area now only a cluster of houses in the beautiful wooded valley leading to the National Trust properties of **Penberth Cove** and part of Treryn Dinas.

The cove is a reminder, perhaps, of the way of life once common in many Cornish fishing communities where wives and children grew violets and narcissi for the London market — now you can

Porthcurno Museum of Submarine Telegraphy

Porthcurno Cove (Trevithick Trust) Displays of historic equipment, guided tours. ☎ (01209) 612142. Open mid-May to October, Monday to Friday, 10am–5pm.

buy wines there. The old trade developed considerably after the opening of Brunel's Royal Albert Bridge in 1859. The valley, cove and headland passed to the National Trust in 1957, many of the small gardens are still cultivated and inshore fishermen are as active as their forefathers were.

The fine jagged headland of **Treryn (Treen) Dinas** forms one side of **Porthcurno**, a bay of startling blues and greens with the Minack Open-air Theatre on its other side. Treryn Fort consists of 36 acres and incorporates a complex of defensive ditches dating from the Iron Age. Here is the famous **Logan Rock**, once moved ill-advisedly by Oliver Goldsmith's nephew for a prank. It weighs 66 tons and the over-enthusiastic young man had to replace it at his own expense. Space is limited on this headland so visitors must leave their cars above the bridge over the stream and walk the last quarter of a mile.

Motorists who leave the B3315 to drive to Porthcurno Beach and on to the **Minack Open-air**

Theatre must be prepared for narrow and winding lanes. The road passes the former Cable and Wireless Training School before the car park nearest to the beach. The building now houses a **Museum of Submarine Telegraphy** which tells of the 14 undersea cables which kept Britain in touch with the Empire. Once the largest international cable station in the world, Porthcurno was also Cornwall's secret underground wartime communications centre.

Theatre-goers have to drive up the steep road beyond to reach their destination, but it is a place not to be missed. It is unique.

In 1932, Miss Rowena Cade and her gardener began the task of creating an amphitheatre out of the natural rock on the cliff edge for a performance of *The Tempest*. Stone seats now replace the original grassy ledges, sound and lighting and dressing-room accommodation are of the best, but the original magic remains. No matter what the play or the players, the setting makes every performance one of individual delight — the sight of the moon rising over the backcloth of ocean is a never-to-be-forgotten experience.

Minack Open-air Theatre

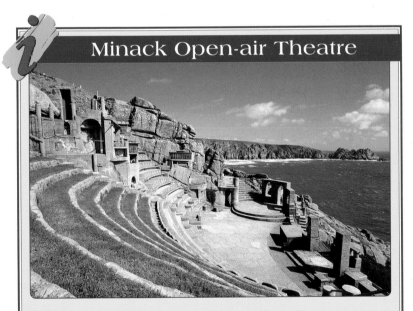

Porthcurno
A unique open-air theatre fashioned from natural rock amphitheatre and the Rowena Cade Exhibition Centre with photographs, models and audio-visual displays. Coffee shop. ☎ (01736) 810694.
Open: 9.30am–5.30pm from April to December daily; 9.30am–4.30pm from October to December.
(Special arrangements on matinée days)

Land's End

Whilst most visitors will approach Land's End by road, there is an alternative for the more energetic. Starting beyond the Minack, from the church of St Levan and its holy well where the road stops, England's most westerly point can be approached on foot. The walk along the coast from here would take most people between two and three hours. On a fine day the views are unrivalled. Here is another place for a whole day's exploration; photographers, botanists, poets and holidaymakers of all ages will find something here to please them.

Longships Lighthouse lies due west of the last group of rocks while seven or eight miles beyond is Wolf Rock. This was the place used by Trinity House for their experiments in airlifting supplies to lighthouse crews. The results were completely successful.

Also at Land's End is one of Cornwall's most varied family attractions. It takes a day to see them all including the Legendary Last Labyrinth, state of the art electronic theatre; Deep Sea Quest and the Air Sea Rescue Experience.

Land's End Holiday Complex

Range of family attractions and exhibitions at the Visitor Centre. Family restaurant and bar. Admission to the landmark conservation area is free.
☎ (01736) 871220.
Open: 10am daily except Christmas Day.

About a mile to the north lies **Sennen**, near the Mayon and Trevescan Cliffs, both National Trust properties. Mayon Cliff is topped with a good example of a Cornish cliff castle (Mayon meaning *maen* or stone) with sheer drops to the sea and a view of basking sharks cruising off the rocks in summer. Above Sennen

Cove, which continues on to Whitesand Bay, is the ancient church of St Sennen, the westernmost church in Britain. It is small and low, as befits its site and was reconsecrated in 1440.

Before the village of **Crows-an-Wra** (Witch's Cross), several paths leave the main road and climb to **Chapel Carn Brea** (not to be confused with Carn Brea at Redruth) which also belongs to the National Trust. It is the first and last hill in Britain and is reputed to have the widest sea view from the mainland of the British Isles. Two Bronze Age barrows and the remains of a medieval chapel dedicated to St Michael may be seen after a gentle climb to the top, where in 1907, one of Cornwall's largest Bronze Age urns was found (it is now in the Truro Museum).

Today at this place, members of St Just Old Cornwall Society light the first in the chain of forty bonfires which illuminate Cornwall on Midsummer Eve from Land's End to the Tamar. This is a particularly festive occasion. Songs and prayers (usually in Cornish) accompany the 'sacrifice' of herbs and flowers thrown in the flames by the Lady of the Flowers to propitiate the sun god; in other words a plea, shared by all visitors, for summer sunshine.

The whole area is good for picnics and walks and for exploring the many nearby antiquities. **Carn Euny** is an ancient Iron Age village now cared for by English

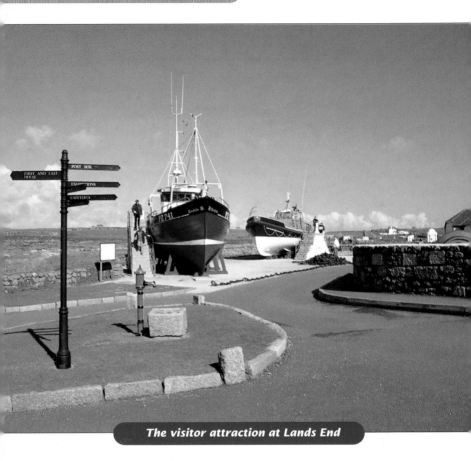

The visitor attraction at Lands End

Heritage. The remains are said to rival those of Chysauster and there is the added attraction of a fine 60ft-long fougou or underground chamber.

Carn Euny Ancient Village

Sancreed
In the care of English Heritage, can be visited at any reasonable time.

Nearby **Sancreed** church is worth looking at. There is a good rood screen, original barrel roofing and five crosses in the churchyard. One, which has lilies on it, is said to be noteworthy. Half hidden in trees in a field close by is the Sancreed holy well and baptistry possessing an exceptional air of mystery and sanctity.

To see the best of the northern part of this peninsula, follow the A3071 out of Penzance. It passes **Castle Horneck** shortly after leaving the edge of the town, a splendid place for a youth hostel and once the home of the Levelis or Lovell family. They owned much of the land in this area in early medieval times and were greatly involved in the Crusades. A well-known Cornish Christmas song, *The Mistletoe Bough*, is based on a tragic incident in the Lovell family. A young bride hid from her husband in an old oak chest and was entombed there, trapped by an unseen spring lock.

The countryside around **St Just** is almost other-worldly; its small fields and dry-stone walls bringing to mind the first men who ever settled here many centuries ago. The tower of the church, though low, can be seen from quite a distance as it has stood in granite solidity since the fifteenth century. Near the clock tower a grassy arena is used today for the ceremony of choosing St Just's Carnival Queen. It is, in fact, a *plen-an-gwary* (Cornish for 'playing place') where medieval mystery plays were performed.

Cape Cornwall Street, which leads from the Square, goes to **Cape Cornwall**, now a National Trust property and a very pleasant spot to spend a day.

Cape Cornwall

1 mile west of St Just
Numerous walks, picnic places and advantageous locations for bird-watching.

The towering nineteenth-century chimney at the summit of Cape Cornwall is a reminder of the many mines once busy in this district. There is an extensive view from this height although

Priest's Cove to the south is probably hidden. It was once a medieval landing beach but now has a different character, and is very popular with local swimmers.

Beyond Land's End is the **Longships Lighthouse** while in the other direction are the picturesque cliff-edge ruins of the Three Crowns Mine at **Botallack**. In 1865, the Prince and Princess of Wales (later King Edward VII and Queen Alexandra) came here and descended the mine. The two engine houses are dramatically situated and worth seeking out.

Pendeen Manor, an attractive sixteenth-century farmhouse, was the birthplace of Dr Borlase, the father of Cornish archaeology. In the yard there is a fougou or underground passage which runs for 23ft in one direction and 33ft in another. At the angle of these is another chamber. There has been much speculation as to the original use of these constructions — Cornwall has several of them. Archaeologists have not yet been able to agree on a satisfactory reason for their existence, so no-one can say whether the fougous were built for storage, defence or even primitive housing. The most recent thought on the subject is that they might have been designed for worship.

Past the manor, the road leads to **Pendeen Watch**, a lighthouse perched on a cliff edge, surrounded by open land where there are birds and flowers in plenty. Built by Trinity House in 1900, its light gives four white flashes every second while the fog signal blasts seven seconds every minute.

Botallack Mine

This view of the Botallack engine houses gives a good impression of the dramatic views from the coastal path near to Lands End

1 mile north of St Just

Ruined mine buildings and arsenic calciner. This profitable mine caught the imagination because it produced riches from beneath the very sea bed itself. Tunnels 7ft by 4ft were cut into a rich copper lode and men worked there each day at a depth of 1,360ft below sea level and half a mile from shore. When the quarterly accounts were produced, owners and mine managers would celebrate their gains with a feast at the Count House.

Pendeen Watch Lighthouse

Fully automated but can still be visited.
(Trevithick Trust)
☎ (01736) 788418.
Open Easter to end of October, Monday to Friday 10am–5pm.

Also at **Pendeen** is **Geevor Mine**. Tin and copper were once brought up from the deep workings of this spectacularly-situated mine, but now it is a mine heritage centre. It was registered as a limited company in 1911 and incorporated the old mines of Wheal Stennack and the ill-fated Levant. Tragedy struck in the latter in 1919 when the beam working the man-engine sheered. The man-engine, carrying its full complement of men and boys to the surface, crashed in ruins to the bottom of the shaft and killed 31 miners. The deeper workings were then abandoned, work ceased altogether from 1930 and the sea eventually broke through into them.

Fortunately the Cornish Engine Preservation Society (now the Trevithick Society) saved the Levant beam engine in 1935 and in 1967 handed it to the National Trust. They then restored both engine and engine house which may be visited on certain days in the summer, a reminder of the prosperous times of 1870 when the area supported about twenty mines. Now only their ruins remain along the cliffs, picturesque and sad, slowly but surely weathering away.

From here to Zennor, the coast road is particularly interesting, especially at **Bosigran** beyond Morvah on the National Trust cliffs. These are wild and exposed but man has learnt how to survive here from prehistoric times, sheltering his crops and animals in tiny fields surrounded by their stone hedges which remain from the Iron Age. The adventurous will probably enjoy the circular walk westwards from Porthmeor Cove to the Iron Age ruins of **Bosigran Castle**, along the spur path past the Climbers' Club hut and back to Porthmeor Cove along the main road.

Geevor Mine

Pendeen (Trevithick Trust)
Ruins of famous tin and copper mine, the last mine to work in Penwith. Museum, surface and underground tours, video presentation. Allow at least 2 hours for site visit and mine tour. Shop and café.
☎ (01736) 788662.
Open: 9.30am–5.30pm, April to October, daily except Saturday. 11am–4pm, November to March, Monday to Friday.

Levant Steam Engine

Trewellard
(National Trust, Trevithick Society and Trevithick Trust)
☎ (01736) 786156.
Open: 11am–5pm July to end September daily except
Saturday, also Easter, May and Spring Bank Holidays;
June – Wednesday, Thursday, Friday and Sunday.

The village of **Porthmeor** is missed by most people who, not unnaturally, are eager to reach Zennor. It is, however, worth asking at Borthpennis for permission to cross the private land and look at the Iron Age village courtyard house here. It is similar in many respects to Chysauster but in addition has its own fortification and gatehouse and is one of the best of the numerous ancient monuments scattered on the downs above the B3306.

Today, **Zennor** is a picturesque miniature village lying in the slight shelter of Trewey Hill. It has, however, a long and interest-

Commando Ridge

Adjoining Bosigran is more National Trust property with a rather special history. Here, during World War II, commandos trained (the western side of the valley is, in fact, named 'Commando Ridge'). Here, too, Lord John Hunt and Sherpa Tensing climbed together to celebrate the tenth anniversary of the ascent of Everest. Never before had Tensing seen the sea and it was his first experience of cliff climbing.

Cars can be parked by the road here and access to the coast is by the spur path previously mentioned.

ing history. Isolated as it was by the natural features of land and sea, Zennor remained almost inaccessible for centuries which is why the presence of the past is still so strong in and around it. The small fields of middle and late Bronze Age settlements are still to be seen at Trewey and Wicca. Some tools and farm implements used for agricultural work down the years are among the exhibits in the small **Wayside Museum**, close to the car park.

Wayside Museum

Zennor, on the St Ives to Land's End coastal road
Exhibits include artifacts connected with the mining, agricultural, quarrying and domestic life of Zennor.
Admission free.
☎ (01736) 796945.
Open: April, daily 11am–5pm; May to September, daily 10am–6pm; October, Sunday to Friday 11am–5pm.

The square church tower is not high but it stands as a clear marker of the centre of Zennor life. On the outside wall of the church just inside the gate is John Davey's memorial stone. He was a man of history who died in 1891 and was said to have been the last one to speak the traditional Cornish language.

There are only two old bench ends in the church but one of them is especially interesting. It portrays a finely carved mermaid and recalls the story of the beautiful sea-creature whose charms were the downfall of Matthew Trewhella. Opposite is the Tinner's Arms, so old that its origins are unknown.

Behind the inn the path, which runs parallel to a trout stream flowing into Pendour (Mermaid) Cove, leads down to Zennor Head. This is part of the 84 acres owned by the National Trust along the cliff, enabling walkers to enjoy the delights of thyme-scented springy turf all the way to Wicca Pool, an Anglo-Saxon name, so out of place in this essentially Cornish area.

There is a great deal to see in this little valley, another Logan Stone, Zennor Quoit, Giant's Rock and the very fine views from the gorse-covered slopes. Little wonder that D.H. Lawrence loved it here and that Virginia Woolf, who spent childhood summers in St Ives, wrote that Cornwall's cliffs and seas had endowed her with riches beyond price.

Nearby, Boswednack Manor is a centre for special interest holidays (☎ 01736 794183 for details about archaeology, bird-watching and natural history).

The quickest way back to Penzance by car is up Trewey Hill, climbing away from Zennor and on to moorland which tempts many to a last walk and picnic above the magnificent cliffs of Penwith's north coast.

7 St Ives and Hayle

Legends cannot be avoided when telling the story of Cornwall. However the one particularly associated with St Ives is usually shrugged off in disbelief, for it is said that the holy St Ia, who was the first to come to this part of the coast, sailed across the water on a leaf!

The idea is very picturesque but seems too extreme to be at all possible — that is, until one remembers the comparatively recent cross-Atlantic voyage, which successfully re-enacted the journey undertaken by St Brendan many centuries ago. A replica of the saint's small craft was made, a mere wooden framework covered with hide and surely as close as could be to the 'leaf' of St Ia.

Arrive by train

Those who are only staying a few hours should leave their cars at Lelant Saltings if they want to see the town in comfort. This avoids parking problems and adds another pleasure for, if the weather is fine, there can be few railway journeys more delightful than the small local train which runs from St Erth to St Ives and collects passengers on the way.

The Tate Gallery and beach at St Ives

There is ample parking space at Lelant and the ride takes a little over 10 minutes, which most people say is all too short because it is probably one of the country's loveliest coastal routes.

From the Saltings, with its interesting estuary scenery, the friendly train takes its passengers along the cliffside to give a clear view of the famous 5-mile stretch of the golden sands which edge the coast from St Ives to Godrevy Point. Vehicular access to the town is restricted during the season, though buses are available from Trenwith car park on the outskirts, so it is both wiser and more pleasant to arrive on the local train. Travel on this in high summer for an unforgettable memory.

The steep, winding cobbled streets of this 'picturesque seaside town par excellence', as it has been called, do much to retain its Cornishness. Looking over the water at Westcott's Quay where the Warren turns into Pednolva Walk, it is easy to understand why the St Ives Art Club decided to hold meetings in that wharfside fishing cellar — the view from there is so characteristic of the whole place. Turner was probably the first artist to come and paint scenes of the town. That was in 1811, but it was Whistler and Sickert who, in 1884, actually established the art colony here. Today's artists exhibit their work in the **Penwith Galleries**.

Penwith Galleries

Back Street West, St Ives
Here is the place to see work of the St Ives Society of Artists — originated by Sir Alfred Munnings.
☎ (01736) 795579.
Open: 10am–1pm and 2.30pm–5pm daily all year except Sundays and Mondays.

Later, in 1927, another group formed, the Society of Artists, which was wider-ranging and included people like Sir Alfred Munnings, Lamorna Birch, Barbara Hepworth and Bernard Leach. Leach, a potter, designed the tiled stone round the grave of Alfred Wallis, the self-taught primitive painter who is buried in Barnoon cemetery beside the car park. In 1920, Leach established a workshop at **Higher Stennack** on the B3306; it is still there and examples of his work are always on display.

Leach Pottery

Higher Stennack
Established by Bernard Leach in 1920. Still used as a pottery. His work is also on display.

Stennack comes from *sten* (Cornish for tin) and the whole valley was once a profitable mining area. The most notable of the workings was probably **Wheal Trenwith**, as it produced not only tin but also copper, pitchblende and the radium used by Madame Curie in her experiments.

Barbara Hepworth lived and worked near the harbour just behind the parish church. Many of her sculptures and paintings are on exhibition permanently since the Tate Gallery bought her studio and garden.

Since World War II other artists went to St Ives and produced work which greatly influenced the development of painting in Britain. As a result a new museum, **The Tate Gallery St Ives**, has opened. Managed by the Tate Gallery it displays local artists' work and is known as the Tate of the West.

Barbara Hepworth Museum and Sculpture Garden

Barnoon Hill, St Ives

Administered by the Tate Gallery, all in the sculptor's former home.

☎ (01736) 796226.

Open April to September, Monday to Saturday 11am–7pm, Sunday 11am–5pm.

October to March, Tuesday to Sunday 11am–5pm.

Tate Gallery

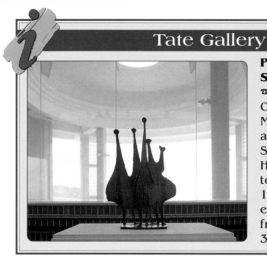

Porthmeor Beach, St Ives

☎ (01736) 796226.
Open: 11am–7pm Monday to Saturday and 11am–5pm Sundays and Bank Holidays from 1 April to 30 September. 11am–5pm daily except Mondays from 1 October to 31 March.

On the island beside St Nicholas' chapel, a huer's hut looks down on the harbour and Smeaton's Pier. In former days, the look-out posted there would watch for pilchards and then cry 'Hevva!' to the waiting fishermen. After a good catch the toast in the town would be to 'Fish, Tin and Copper'.

St Ives Museum

Wheal Dream
Local history.
☎ (01736) 796005.
Open: May to October, Monday to Friday 10am–5pm. Saturday 10am–4pm. Some Sundays 2pm–4.30pm.

It is strange to see animal traps on show but one of these could trap three mice inside at once and this is a strong clue to the reason for the local preference for cats. St Ives is known for two types of cat. One is short-backed and stubby-legged, the other a large,

contented animal resembling Alice in Wonderland's Cheshire cat. It was no doubt the local interest in cats that probably accounted for the nursery rhyme that helps many youngsters learn to count, 'As I was going to St Ives'.

A large part of the main room is devoted to exhibits connected with John Knill (1733–1811), perhaps the most memorable of all St Ives' citizens. Customs officer, mayor, lawyer and lovable wealthy eccentric, Knill was at one time private secretary to the Earl of Buckingham and a trustee of his estate.

Rumour has it that he was also a privateer, and he did have plenty of opportunity for this. On his instructions John Smeaton built the harbour pier which provided such necessary shelter for shipping, and Knill built the Steeple monument just outside the town. He intended this to be his final resting place but he was buried in London. In his will he laid down that every 5 years there was to be a ceremony held on 25 July when ten girls and two widows should dance round the Steeple. A strange request but one which has kept his memory alive.

Five splendid sandy beaches which can accommodate many people, form a golden crescent round the town. On one of them — or perhaps all — Virginia Woolf played when she was on holiday at Talland House and later brought these early memories of Godrevy into *To The Lighthouse*. Today St Ives, with its cliff walks, wind-surfing, fishing and sailing, still welcomes visitors to the essential Cornish atmosphere which people so enjoy.

The train returns from a small station above Porthminster Beach and as it moves away, Tregenna Castle Hotel, one of Cornwall's finest, with its castellated turrets, may be glimpsed high above on the cliff top.

The next stop is **Carbis Bay** which has such fine, smooth sands that it is perhaps the most popular of all the local beaches. This is in sharp contrast to the appearance it had in the last century when it was used as a dump for mining waste.

Lelant is an unexpected place with a quiet individuality that has to be searched for. This probably stems from the knowledge that it was a thriving seaport in the Middle Ages, long before St Ives achieved popularity. The church lies behind the Saltings in a village of old-world charm. It is dedicated to St Uny and was the parish church for St Ives as well until 1826. Inside are interesting memorials to members of the Praed family from Trevethoe, the mansion at the foot of Trencrom.

William Praed (1620) and his family are remembered in a slate carving, with kneeling figures, flowers, sand-glass and skull. His famous descendants are Mackworth (whose portrait is in the St Ives Museum) and William. The former was the eminent engineer who planned England's canal system, the latter, the

Porthminster Beach

banker after whom London's Praed Street is named. Another building of the past is the abbey in Lower Lelant, a long, low sixteenth-century construction, and L-shaped as befits the period. Neither Trevethoe nor the abbey are open to the public.

The St Ives branch line ends at **St Erth** which is another example of a once proud and busy place. The Star Inn was there in the seventeenth century when the Trewinnards startled everyone by introducing the first private coach to Cornwall. Truro Museum now has that same vehicle in its safe keeping.

Most drivers hurry through **Hayle,** glad when they are beyond it, but its present dullness does, in fact, hide one of Cornwall's oldest ports. Now the estuary provides sanctuary for birds and there is a bird reserve with a viewing hide.

Lelant Bird Reserve

Quay House
Overlooking the Hayle estuary, an open hide is available in the grounds of Quay House.

This particular estuary has been important since Bronze Age times when copper and gold were sent from Ireland to Brittany via St Michael's Mount. Centuries later, when the Industrial Revolution demanded the best in engineering, this part of the world provided it.

The old wharves, still visible near the railway bridge, were once part of the great foundry and engineering business belonging to Harvey's — known throughout the world simply as 'Harvey's of Hayle'. Beside the B3302, which leads out of the square and up Foundry Hill, are some remains of this once extensive complex — the hammer mill and the old mill pond can still be found. Those who designed the town's modern purpose-built library were (fortunately) determined that Hayle's great past should not entirely be forgotten and now, for all to see, on its gable are three original wood patterns for gear wheels for mining machines made in Harvey's foundry in the late 1880s. Harvey's made the largest steam engine in the world — with a 12 feet diameter cylinder. It survives in Holland.

Today that secondary road makes its way to a more modern concept — **Paradise Park.** Here is a fine collection of the world's rarest and most beautiful birds, including flamingoes, toucans and free-flying parrots. Within the grounds there is also the new Cornish otter sanctuary, an ambitious conservation scheme to help restore the otter to the local countryside.

Another project, probably even closer to Cornish hearts, is 'Operation Chough'. Launched here in 1987 it is one stage in a 3-year study into the possibility of re-establishing the chough in selected locations on the coast. This rare bird which, with its red beak and legs, was once a familiar sight on Cornwall's rugged cliffs, is associated with King Arthur and so synonymous with Cornwall that it appears on the County Council's coat of arms. Detailed research has been done in other Celtic parts of Britain and results already show that the chough's decline is closely linked to the disappearance of the Large Blue butterfly.

It would be wrong to leave Hayle without remembering a person who was born in the town and whose name is as internationally famous today as Harvey's was in the last century. She was Florence Nightingale Graham, born in 1884, one of the three children of a chemist who encouraged her experiments with cosmetics.

The Graham family anticipated the collapse of Cornish mining and in 1908 emigrated to Canada. Young Florence soon moved to New York, and became a partner in a beauty salon business but before long, opened her own beauty parlour on Fifth Avenue. She took the name of Elizabeth Arden from the novels, *Elizabeth and her German Garden* and *Enoch Arden*. In 1915 she introduced mascara and eye-shadow and eventually extended her business to thirty-five countries. She also achieved another first when she opened her health farms. Though she died in 1966 the company she founded continues to thrive.

Copperhouse, now an extension of Hayle, has only the Copperhouse Inn sign and, by the old quay, walls built of dark green copper-slag blocks, to serve as a reminder of its former importance as a copper smelting site. Across the Hayle Canal, the romantically named church at

Paradise Park

Hayle
Collection of the world's rarest birds, otter sanctuary.
☎ (01736) 757407.
Open 10am–5pm, May to September, daily; 10am–4pm rest of year, daily.

Phillack (St Felicitas) overlooks the water and nearby is Riviere House where Compton Mackenzie and his sister, the actress, Fay Compton, spent many happy childhood holidays.

The huge stretch of towans (sand dunes) which forms part of St Ives Bay is ideal for holiday-makers to walk, swim, or laze, although all lifeguard's warnings must be observed. **Connor Downs** is a sprawling development beside the A30 above Gwithian and many historians think it possible that the ancient city of Connor (Irish for 'haven') lies there beneath the dunes.

Gwithian itself is a small village with a low-towered fifteenth-century church. The unusual sight of thatch here makes it an artist's delight: animal lovers, however, take pleasure in watching the seals which are sometimes seen at Navax Point (belonging to the National Trust) beyond **Godrevy Lighthouse**. The cliffs all round here are turfy and good for walking, but bathers will find that the water is often stained by the Red River which collects tin waste on its way to the sea.

GETTING THERE

By Air

Brymon Airways, a wholly-owned subsidiary of British Airways, operates four flights a day between London Gatwick and Newquay airport, ☎ 0345 222111. Flights are available from Dublin and Cork to Plymouth (☎ 0345 446447) and from Belfast, Dublin, Guernsey and Jersey to Exeter (☎ 0990 676676). Car hire is available at the airports.

By Road

The M4, M5 and M6 motorways have made travel to Cornwall simple and straightforward, while within Cornwall itself, the two major holiday routes, the A30 and A38 continue to improve, with fast dual carriageways as far as Bodmin and most of the way to Penzance. If you enter Cornwall via North Devon, then there is the Atlantic Highway, the A39, which you can join at junction 27 on the M5.

By Coach

National Express offers direct services from London, the South-East, the North-East, the Midlands and from Yorkshire. The service from London Victoria and Heathrow Airport runs six times a day ☎ (0990) 010104.

By Rail

National Rail Enquiries – train times and fares information ☎ (0345) 484950.

Great Western provide services from London, Reading, South Wales, the Cotswolds and the West Country, bookings ☎ (0345) 000125.

Wales and West Passenger Trains run direct services into Cornwall via Bristol, from Manchester, Birmingham, Bath, Swindon and Cardiff. Truro, St Ives and Falmouth are all easily accessible by train ☎ (0345) 125625.

Virgin Trains operate services from Birmingham, Bristol, the North and Scotland, ☎ (0345) 222333.

The Cornish Holiday Experience offers fully inclusive rail holiday packages. Bookings and information ☎ (0800) 7313261.

ACCOMMODATION

A wide range of all types of accommodation, from camping and caravan sites, self-catering flats and cottages, youth hostels, family holiday parks, bed and breakfast establishments to luxury hotels, is available in West Cornwall. Full details available from the Tourist Information Centres listed in this Fact File.

If your local Tourist Information Centre is part of the Booking Agency, they will be able to book accommodation for you with the TICs in West Cornwall.

Holiday Cottages

If you wish to rent accommodation, we suggest you telephone either:

Cornish Cottage Holidays,
The Old Turnpike Dairy,
Godolphin Road, Helston,
Cornwall TR13 8QL
☎ 01326 573808
Fax 01326 564992
e-mail: CCH@olddairy.demon.co.uk

Cornish Traditional Cottage Co,
Blisland,
Bodmin,
Cornwall PL30 4HS
☎ 01208 821666
Fax 01208 821766
e-mail ggo99@dial.pipex.com

The **Youth Hostels Association** has plenty of rooms in Cornwall, for those travelling independently or for those wishing a family room. Contact YHA, Via Gellia Mill, Bonsall, Matlock, Derbyshire DE4 2XA, ☎ 01629 825850, Fax 01629 824571, e-mail yhaenglishregions@compuserve.com

In 1999 YHA is establishing a central booking service for the South-West Coastal Path, between Minehead and Swanage.
Contact YHA Central Reservation Service, PO Box 67, Matlock, Derbyshire, DE4 3YX, ☎ 01629 581061, Fax 01629 581062
e-mail centralreservations.yha.org.uk

BIRD WATCHING

West Cornwall is one of Britain's best sites for watching seabirds. There is also a good variety of inland birds and the possibility of rare species that have been blown off course during storms. Recommended viewing points are:

Sea birds
Godrevy Point; The Island, St Ives; Pendeen Lighthouse; Gwennap Head; the Promenade from Newlyn to Penzance.

Inland
West Penwith Moors especially inland from the B3306 between Gurnards Head and Morvah.

Wading birds
Hayle estuary; Marazion marsh.

Water fowl
Drift reservoir west of Newlyn.

For up-to-the-minute information on birds in the area ☎ (0891) 884500.

CYCLING

There are few designated off-road cycle routes in West Cornwall but two suggestions would be:

Near St Agnes the **Tehidy Country Park Trail** has over three miles of cycle paths, ☎ (01209) 714494 for details.

The **Portreath Tramroad** (from Portreath to Crofthandy) offers over eight miles of cycling suitable for mountain bikes. This is managed by Groundwork Kerrier who can advise on routes. Parking is available at Groundwork Kerrier, Old Cowlins Mill, Penallick, Carn Brea, Redruth, TR15 3YR where mountain bikes can be hired. Cycle hire is available in most towns.

Fact File

DOGS

Dogs are banned from many beaches in West Cornwall because of the risk to health from fouling. Visitors should check before allowing a dog on to a beach.

FACILITIES FOR THE DISABLED

Where possible the availability of facilities for the disabled at particular attractions has been indicated in the text. For more detailed information contact: **The Cornwall Disability Information and Advice Network**, ☎ (01736) 751300. Advice on holidays, accessibility and hire of equipment. **Cornwall Disabled Association**, ☎ (01872) 273518

FISHING

There are excellent opportunities for all types of fishing in West Cornwall: deep sea fishing, boat angling, fly fishing, coarse fishing, rock fishing, beach fishing. Tackle shops are abundant and are very good sources of information about local fishing of all kinds.

Deep Sea Fishing
Boat trips are available from Penzance, Mevagissey, Falmouth, Hayle and St Ives for full day, half day or evening deep sea fishing. Details are available at the harbour side or from local tackle shops.

Boat Angling
There are boat launching facilities at most harbours but permission should always be sought from the harbourmaster, as should local advice on weather and sea conditions.

Fly Fishing
Argal Reservoir
West of Falmouth. Fly fishing, picnic area. 1 April to 31 October. ☎ (01579) 342366

Stithians Reservoir
About four miles west of Penryn. Open season April to October ☎ (01209) 860301

Drift Reservoir
Three miles west of Penzance on A30. 65 acres. Season 1 April to 12 October. ☎ (01736) 363869

Coarse Fishing
Bolingey Lake
Nr. Perranporth
All year, ☎ (01872) 572388.

Boscathnoe
Nr. Penzance
All year, ☎ (01392) 443362

Bussow
Nr. St Ives
☎ (01837) 871565

Digging for bait is now banned from a number of harbours and estuaries. Consult local tackle shops for information about this and where to fish and obtain licences or permits if necessary. Always take local advice when fishing at the coast, either on shore or from a boat, as the area can be affected by heavy Atlantic swells even in the height of summer.

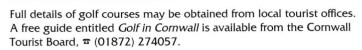

GOLF

Full details of golf courses may be obtained from local tourist offices.
A free guide entitled *Golf in Cornwall* is available from the Cornwall
Tourist Board, ☎ (01872) 274057.

MAPS

The best maps to use are Ordnance Survey Landranger Series 2cm to 1 km
1:50,000 numbers 203, 204; Ordnance Survey Explorer Series 4cm to
1km 1:25,000 numbers 102, 103, 104, 105.

PUBLIC TRANSPORT IN THE AREA

Locally, an extensive network of bus services is run by a number of
operators. Timetable information is available from **Western National**
☎ (01209) 719988 and **Truronian Travel** ☎ (01872) 273453.

The *Cornwall Public Transport Timetable* covering bus, ferry, plane and
train is available at £1.60 (inc. pp) from Passenger Transport Unit, County
Hall, Truro, Cornwall TR1 3AY ☎ (01872) 322142.

☎ (01209) 719988 for details of co-ordination of rail and bus services at
stations.

Wales and West passenger trains offer many scenic rides within Cornwall
and Truro, St Ives and Falmouth are all easily accessible by train
☎ (0345) 125625.

There are helicopter flights (20 minute flight) to the Isles of Scilly daily
except Sunday, from Penzance Heliport. British International Helicopters
☎ (01736) 363871.

A fixed-wing air service (15 minute flight) operates all year, Monday to
Saturday to the Isles of Scilly from Land's End. A similar service operates
from Newquay but with a reduced service in the winter months. Isles of
Scilly Travel Centre ☎ (0345) 105555.

The sea crossing to the Isles of Scilly on Scillonian III leaves from Penzance
and takes two and a half hours.
Isles of Scilly Travel Centre ☎ (0345) 105555.

ROCK CLIMBING

West Cornwall is the foremost sea cliff climbing area in Britain with the
most popular cliffs being found at Bosigran, Sennen and Chair Ladder.
There are granite, greenstone and killas cliffs offering climbs from Difficult
to E8 grade for the experienced climber. It is essential that climbers
remember that these cliffs are affected by tidal movements and that
Atlantic swells can hit the cliffs with explosive force, even in summer.
Great care should be taken at all times.

It is also important to bear in mind environmental considerations concerning flora and fauna, especially at bird nesting sites. A free booklet *The Green Guide* is available from the British Mountaineering Council. The used of fixed gear such as bolts or drilled pegs is not acceptable here.

British Mountaineering Council South West ☎ (01179) 542425
National Trust Countryside Manager (West Penwith) ☎ (01736) 796993
The National Trust owns many of the climbing cliffs.

Climbing courses/guiding
Compass West, operate June to September ☎ (01736) 871447

SAILING

All types of sailing are available from small dinghies to sea cruising, creek hopping to voyages to France and Ireland, and excellent facilities abound in West Cornwall. Many yacht clubs offer temporary membership to visitors. Amongst the many available are:

Helford River Sailing Club ☎ (01326) 231460
Newquay Sailing Club ☎ (01637) 878574
Pentewan Sands Sailing Club ☎ (01726) 817704
Royal Cornwall Yacht Club ☎ (01326) 311105
St Mawes Sailing Club ☎ (01326) 270686

Visitors' moorings are available at most harbours, contact the appropriate harbourmaster.

TOURIST INFORMATION CENTRES

Further information on any specific activity or event may be obtained from the appropriate Tourist Information Office.

Falmouth
28 Killigrew Street
☎ (01209) 611102 or
(01326) 312300

Helston
79 Meneage Street
☎ (01326) 565431

Newquay
Marcus Hill
☎ (01637) 871345

Penzance
Station Approach
☎ (01736) 362207

Perranporth
☎ (01872) 573368

St Austell
By-Pass Service Station,
Southbourne Road
☎ (01726) 76333

St Ives
The Guildhall, Street An Pol
☎ (01736) 796297

Truro
Municipal Building,
Boscawen Street
☎ (01872) 274555

WALKING

Coastal walking is excellent in West Cornwall but there are opportunities to explore inland as well. Here you will find heritage trails, pilgrim routes and riverside walks as well as wild moors with ancient sites to visit.

The South West Way long distance footpath runs for some 185 miles around the coast of West Cornwall. Many sections can be walked as day walks, using public transport to return to base in the evening. The South West Way Association produce a guide to the route with details of accommodation, transport, ferries and tide tables.

South West Way Association ☎ (01803) 873061
Passenger Transport Unit, Cornwall County Council ☎ (01872) 322142

Further information on walking in West Cornwall may be obtained from:
The Cornwall Tourist Board, ☎ (01872) 274057

The National Trust ☎ (01208) 74281

and all local tourist offices.

WATERSPORTS

Facilities for Bodyboarding, Surfing, Windsurfing, Canoeing and Diving are excellent in West Cornwall. The Cornwall Tourist Board, ☎ (01872) 274057, can supply very good information on all aspects of watersports. It is essential that those who are new to these activities and to the area seek local advice in order to undertake the sports safely.

Surfing
British Surfing Association ☎ (01736) 331077
Surf Line (for sea conditions) ☎ (0839) 360360

Canoeing
Colin Rule, British Canoe Union, St Austell ☎ (01726) 72901

Diving
British Sub-Aqua Club (local branch) ☎ (01288) 353714
Bill Bowen (Penzance) ☎ (01736) 752135
Cornish Diving Services (Falmouth) ☎ (01326) 311265

WEATHER

West Cornwall is a very narrow peninsula and the weather is much influenced by the sea. In winter, temperatures rarely fall below 0°C and thanks to the Gulf Stream the area is usually warmer than the rest of mainland Britain. The driest months are likely to be in early summer and May tends to be the sunniest. The weather here can change very quickly and sunshine is never very far away.

Weatherline ☎ (0891) 600256
Marine Call ☎ (0891) 500458

INDEX

LANDMARK
Publishing Ltd ● ● ● ●

VISITORS GUIDES

* Practical guides for the independent traveller
* Written in the form of touring itineraries
* Full colour illustrations and maps
* Detailed Landmark FactFile of practical information
* Landmark Visitors Guides highlight all the interesting places you will want to see, so ensuring that you make the most of your visit

1. *Britain*

Cornwall	Jersey
Cotswolds &	Lake District
Shakespeare	Peak District
Country	Scotland
Devon	Somerset
Dorset	South Devon
East Anglia	Southern Lakeland
Guernsey	Southern Peak District
Hampshire	Yorkshire Dales
Harrogate	York

2. *Europe*

Bruges	Provence
Cracow	Riga
Italian Lakes	Vilnius
Madeira	

3. *Other*

Dominican Republic
Florida: Gulf Coast
Florida Keys
India: Goa
India: Kerala
  & The South
New Zealand
Orlando &
  Central Florida
St Lucia
The Gambia

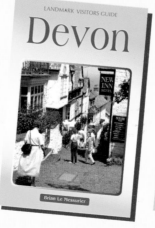

Landmark Publishing
Waterloo House, 12 Compton, Ashbourne, Derbyshire DE6 IDA England
Tel: 01335 347349 Fax: 01335 347303 e-mail: landmark@clara.net

Published by
Landmark Publishing Ltd,
Waterloo House, 12 Compton, Ashbourne, Derbyshire DE6 1DA England
Tel: 01335 347349 Fax: 01335 347303 e-mail: landmark@clara.net

1st Edition
ISBN 1 901 522 24 5

Print: UIC Printing & Packaging Pte Ltd, Singapore

Cartography: James Allsopp

Design: Samantha Witham

Editor: Kay Coulson

Front Cover: Land's End
Back cover, top: Trellisick Gardens, near Feock
Back cover, bottom: Pendennis Castle, Falmouth

Picture Credits

**All photographs are supplied by Lindsey Porter
except the following:
Carrick District Council:** 44, 41 both, 42
The Minack Theatre: 71
Tate Gallery St Ives: 80/81, 83, 84 ˙
Penwith District Council: 2, 85
The late Geoff Irving: 44